FORGET ABOUT
LOCATION,
LOCATION,
LOCATION!

FORGET ABOUT
LOCATION,
LOCATION,
LOCATION!

THE DEFINITIVE REAL ESTATE INVESTMENT GUIDE

OZZIE JUROCK

REVISED EDITION

Stoddart

First edition published in 1999 by Jurock Publishing Ltd.

Revised edition published in 2000 by Stoddart Publishing Co. Limited
34 Lesmill Road, Toronto, Canada M3B 2T6
180 Varick Street, 9th Floor, New York, New York 10014

Distributed in Canada by:
General Distribution Services Ltd.
325 Humber College Blvd., Toronto, Ontario M9W 7C3
Tel. (416) 213-1919   Fax (416) 213-1917
Email cservice@genpub.com

Distributed in the United States by:
General Distribution Services Inc.
PMB 128, 4500 Witmer Industrial Estates, Niagara Falls, New York 14305-1386
Toll-free Tel.1-800-805-1083   Toll-free Fax 1-800-481-6207
Email gdsinc@genpub.com

04 03 02 01 00 1 2 3 4 5

Canadian Cataloguing in Publication Data
Jurock, Ozzie
Forget about location, location, location!: the definitive real estate investment guide
Rev. ed.
ISBN 0-7737-6111-X
1. Real estate investment. I. Title. II. Title: Location, location, location!
HD 1382.5.J87 2000   332.63'24   C00-930028-7

U.S. Cataloguing in Publication Data
Jurock, Ozzie.
Forget about location, location, location!:
the definitive real estate investment guide / Ozzie Jurock.
[264]p.: cm.
Originally published: Vancouver, B.C.: Jurock Publishing, 1999.
Includes index.
Summary: The new focus in real estate investment based on timing and trends.
ISBN 0-7737-6111-X (pbk.)
1. Real estate investment. 2. Finance, Personal. I. Title. 332.63/24 21 2000 CIP

Cover Design: Bill Douglas @ The Bang
Text Design: Tannice Goddard

THE CANADA COUNCIL | LE CONSEIL DES ARTS
FOR THE ARTS | DU CANADA
SINCE 1957 | DEPUIS 1957

*We acknowledge for their financial support of our
publishing program the Canada Council, the Ontario Arts
Council, and the Government of Canada through the
Book Publishing Industry Development Program (BPIDP).*

Printed and bound in Canada

For my wife, Jo;
our children, Liesl and Marc;
our grandchildren, Maximillian, Fraser, and Remy;
my brother, Dieter, and his wife, Biggi;
my nieces and nephews, Deborah, Lea, Pascal, and Frederik;
my wife's sister, Victoria, and my son's wife, Kelly.

A happy family is but an earlier heaven.
— JOHN BOWRING

Contents

Introduction

Man has his future within him, dynamically alive at this present moment.
— Abraham Maslow

Iknow from personal experience that investing in real estate can be one of the most exhilarating adventures of life. Throughout my career, I have worked as a real estate salesperson, a branch manager, and eventually as president of Royal LePage (Residential). As a private investor, I have sold, bought, owned, and managed properties too numerous to count. That's a lot of real estate over a lot of years, and during that time I have developed a few theories about what sells and what doesn't, what to buy and what not to, and how to keep out of trouble.

Well, being the nice guy I am, I wanted to share what I had learned with others. And so I began publishing my weekly and monthly news-letters — *Jurock's Facts by Fax* and *Jurock's Real Estate Investor* — and offering investor outlook seminars. Yet even after receiving one of my newsletters or attending one of my seminars, people would often say to me, "Ozzie, where can I go to learn more?" Most colleges, real estate boards, and even financial institutions offer some kind of basic course in buying and selling real estate, to be sure. And many successful investors (myself included) sell audio- and videotapes that furnish tips for those just starting out. And then, of course, there are the late-night TV courses (avoid these!) and countless organized investment clubs (some are good, some are bad). But none of these quite seemed to fit the bill. What is needed, I thought to myself, is not a one-shot course or tape, but a more detailed, sophisticated manual that investors can refer to again and again and again. And that is when I decided to write *Forget about Location, Location, Location!*

Now, don't get me wrong. I'm not suggesting that this book alone will tell you everything you need to know about investing in real estate. No book I've ever read can teach you the intangibles, for example, such as how to get a feel for a property or a property owner, or how to weed out the bad tenants from the good. No, the only way you'll really learn everything is to get out there and do it. If you want experience writing offers, get out there and write some. If you want to understand how to research and do due diligence, start at the bottom and learn as you go. Eventually, often through trial and error, you will turn yourself from a novice investor into an expert.

I do believe, however, that this book can make that journey a little less rocky (and hopefully full of a lot of trial but very little error). What I have tried to do here is provide you with a good, solid foundation from which to start. That's why the book begins with the basics, what I like to call real estate's Ten Commandments: what, where, when, why, how much, how, how long, what to watch for, who to trust, and if. Whether you're a beginner, a master, or somewhere in between, you need a good grounding in these principles before you can start to even think about buying.

Once I have taken you through the basics, I turn my attention to what I believe is the biggest myth in the real estate market today: that the only three things that matter are location, location, location. I show you instead two much more important principles of investing — timing and trend analysis — and I introduce you to several factors that can help you decide when and where to buy. These factors include things like inflation, supply and demand, migration, and prospects for growth.

Of course, understanding these determining factors is of little use unless you also understand yourself and your investment objectives. That is why I recommend taking a good, hard look at yourself from a variety of perspectives — financial, intellectual, and temperamental. Are you a keeper or a flipper? How involved do you want to be with your properties? What is your tolerance for risk? Are you trying to build a portfolio of income-producing properties, or are you simply looking to buy a second home for its rental income? I teach you the importance of having a written investment plan, the power of positive thinking, and how to think big even if you're buying small.

Once I have shown you the path to greater self-awareness, I get down to the nitty-gritty: buying, selling, negotiating tactics, and the reality of the realty marketplace. And because that marketplace isn't always a friendly spot to be, I alert you to some of the most common-place scams and hoaxes, and I warn you of the pitfalls sometimes associated with REITs and limited partnerships. I even tell you how you can (if you want to) take advantage of other people's misfortune.

Finally, I review some of the details you must consider once you have decided to buy: how to find reliable and knowledgeable advisers, how to manage your properties as efficiently and painlessly as possible, and how to arrange your affairs so you're paying the least amount of tax possible. Then I close with what I believe are two of the most valuable chapters in the entire book: a recap of what to buy and what to avoid, and a brief synopsis of what to do when trouble comes knocking at your door.

So what does it all amount to in the end? Well, I want this book to make you aware of how vast in scope the real estate investment game truly is. The key to being a successful player is to educate yourself, and I hope this book will be the first step in that process. But don't just read it once and then put it on the shelf. Keep it close at hand, so you can refer to it time and again. I truly believe you'll get something new with each new reading. It will bring to light things you've overlooked and remind you of things you've forgotten.

But most of all, I want this book to teach you that this game isn't difficult to play. You don't need to be rich, brilliant, or even lucky to be successful at it. All it takes is hard work, patience, resourcefulness, and self-awareness. And as this book will show, these are qualities anyone can master.

1

The Basics

If the basics were really basic, we wouldn't have to write so much about them.

This chapter is mostly about money and what to do with it. (I'm assuming that you want to do something with your money to make it grow. If you don't, then I can tell you what to do with it in two words: spend it.) Let's imagine that you have wads of money piled up in front of you, and you want to do something to make that pile even bigger. What should that something be?

Well, there is no shortage of people who would be more than happy to tell you that. It's amazing, in fact, how we're constantly bombarded by an endless stream of predictions and recommendations from financial planners, banks, trust companies — you name it. And because most of us react quickly to fear, fear-mongering is their most popular technique. We are told that the pension plan we are depending on won't be there for us when we need it. And even if it is, we are told, its purchasing power will be practically nil. You begin to imagine yourself differently: grey, wizened, bent with age, warming up a can of dog food for your supper as the wind blows through the cracked window of your one-room hovel. You are told that if you have an income of $50,000 now, you will need a portfolio of $10 million to enjoy the same standard of living when you retire in twenty years. The closer you get to retirement, the more your fear will grow.

But do any of the so-called experts really know what they're talking about? If you had followed the best advice available twenty years ago, you would have locked yourself into a plan that was guaranteed to remit what was then considered the "safe amount" of $500 per month for the rest of your life (a lot back then — pocket change today). Imagine the desperate poverty you would retire to today if you had only $500 a month. Stone soup would be a luxury.

We need more money now — that much is certain. But who knows what money will be worth tomorrow. Is there anyone who can say for sure what will happen to interest rates and inflation? Will the supercharged stocks and mutual funds of today still be outperforming in five, ten, or fifteen years? Will the so-called New World Order bring wealth and prosperity or poverty and want? Who among us can possibly know the state of the world three months from now — much less twenty years from now? It's just not possible.

However, in the turmoil of all this sound and fury, one asset has weathered the changes. Had you bought good-quality real estate three decades ago, you would not be concerned about your future today. That real estate would have kept up with inflation, remained secure, and steadily appreciated in value. Sure, there would have been some temporary dips — real estate, after all, is cyclical in nature. But over the years, the base value of real estate has been steadily increasing. And that property you bought thirty years ago would today be paid off and clear — which means either a mortgage-free home (no more monthly "rent" payments to the bank) or a steady rental income courtesy of your tenants. Simply put, if you place a good portion of your assets into real estate today, you won't have to worry about tomorrow.

APPRECIATING APPRECIATION

Home ownership (the most common form of real estate holding) has been the single largest factor in the accumulation of wealth for the average North American. And that accumulation of wealth is largely a result of straight appreciation due to inflation. The basic principle of appreciation holds true for pretty well any healthy major urban centre, but to get a real sense of how it works, let's take a look at Vancouver, B.C., as an example.

In 1960, the average Vancouver home sold for $13,105. Forty years later, in 2000, the average sale price was $295,000. That's almost a 2,260 percent return! If you had made a 10 percent down payment of $1,310, you would at this point be gloating over a 22,600 percent return, and you would have a free-and-clear roof over your head.

So what does all this mean for today's buyer? Well, if the laws of mathematics are not repealed, in the year 2039 the average Vancouver home could sell for — you'd better sit down for this one — $6.7 million! You *must* be on the appreciation conveyor belt. If you're not, you're going to be left so far behind that it will be financially disastrous.

Of course, when you combine appreciation with leverage, you will have unlocked the great secret of achieving optimum results with your investment. When your gain is measured in terms of the capital invested, not the actual price of the property, the results are astounding. Let's say, for instance, that you buy a million-dollar home for $100,000 down. If the house price rises to $2 million, that's an increase of 100 percent on the house but 1000 percent on your investment.

But the real estate game is not as simple as it used to be. In fact, its only constant is that everything is always changing. The secret of surviving and prospering in the game is being able to adapt to the changes.

The 1980s, for example, were very forgiving for the amateur. If you had a few dollars back then, you could buy any piece of real estate, anywhere, and you would make money. Even if you were utterly brainless, it was almost impossible to make a big enough mistake. If you paid too much, it often only meant that you had bought a little too soon. Thanks to inflation, prices soon caught up to you and bailed you out.

But after the 1980s, the real estate world became less forgiving. For some investors, the times were downright terrifying. Markets fluctuated area by area, in terms of both volume of sales and prices. Different real estate categories rose or fell without any apparent logic. You could see the average single-family detached home rise in value by 40 percent in one market area while downtown condos slumped in value by 12 to 20 percent in the exact same area.

The people who tried to play by the old rules soon found themselves playing someone else's game. And most of the time, they were handed their heads. Was it possible to avoid the dangers and prosper? Yes, but you had to put aside the old-fashioned belief in location, location, location, and instead read the trends, take advantage of timing, and implement some new techniques.

UNDERSTANDING THE NEW CONSUMER

To be successful real estate investors, we must first learn to understand ourselves. That means we have to understand our investment objectives in relation to the risks we are willing and able to tolerate. We then must understand that aspect of ourselves that is part of what I like to call the new consumer. Learning what motivates the new consumer is important because that is what will tell us how he or she is likely to act and react in any given situation.

But the "talk people talk" is different from the "walk people walk." Buyers are liars. They say one thing and then go out and do the opposite.

If you take a poll, for example, people will tell you that they want service and human interaction when satisfying their consumer needs, but they blithely drive by the local corner store to the superstore with the mountain of goods piled to the ceiling. Then they load up with a twenty-seven-year supply of pink toilet paper (it was such a deal), haul it out to their hulking off-road vehicle that cost more than a Cadillac but will never see a mud splatter in its life, and celebrate the five dollars they saved on the toilet paper with a six-dollar no-fat double latte and an almond biscotti (in other words, coffee and a cookie).

The new consumer will drive miles out of his way and circle parking lots endlessly — all to save five cents on a can of soup. But he will also splurge fifty dollars for a bottle of wine with a superb aroma. There are lessons here for all businesses, not just real estate. Consumers today will spend big for something they perceive as unique and special.

But remember, most consumers would have drawn you a much different picture. So you have to be careful when you're evaluating the prognostications of the pollsters, demographers, and economists. What people say and what they do are two very different things. Learn to separate the myth from the reality.

Still, one thing is for sure: we are different from how we used to be. The pre-, post-, and current baby boomers each want a certain type of home and a certain lifestyle, and the degree to which you can accurately read these trends will determine how well you prosper in your real estate investments. Savvy investors will ask the right questions and get the right answers before they make their investment decisions.

So what other consumer trends should investors watch? Well, the new consumer is concerned with living a longer and healthier life. As a result, a whole new philosophy of physical behaviour is developing. We cram ourselves with oat bran, devour lettuce and spinach by the bale, and torture ourselves with jogging and other assorted masochisms. Some of us do it for an improved quality of life; most of us do it in a misguided and vain attempt to slow the clock. Unfortunately, we do not have the same dedication when it comes to cramming real know-how into our heads. We'd rather have someone else do the thinking for us.

What we really need to do — in concert with exercising our bodies — is exercise our minds and direct our thinking towards the basic principles of life. Do this and you will create in yourself the resilience, self-reliance, and security that you are looking for and that no financial planner can give you. In the words of Frank Ogden, Dr. Tomorrow: "In the past we were a nation of haves and have-nots; in the future we'll be a nation of knows and know-nots." Make sure you're one of the knows. Make life an ongoing journey of personal growth of mind and body, and no matter where the world goes you will be safe.

But what, you may be asking, does this have to do with real estate investment? Go back and reread the previous paragraph — it is one of the most important of this entire book! The point behind it is this: before you invest in property, invest in yourself. Time, thought, and action all help to create opportunity. Inertia, sloth, and the unwillingness to roll up your mental sleeves and work hard insulate you from opportunity and open you to mistakes. I know people who spend more time analyzing the fine print on a can of tomato juice than they do reading the fine print on an investment prospectus or examining a house before they buy it.

Successful real estate investing is like anything else. It requires work, imagination, and individual enterprise. But you've got to do the *important* work yourself. There is no way around it. I do not know of any successful investor in real estate (other than the homeowner, happily and unwittingly riding up the escalator of inflation) who hasn't learned the ins and outs of the business, and who doesn't actively and consistently scour the marketplace, make offers, and when they are accepted, personally do the due diligence.

The opportunities are everywhere, and successful investors don't have to have any qualities that average folks don't have. All successful investors follow the same guidelines, while the unsuccessful ones find their own special ways to get into trouble. However — and this is a biggie — consistently successful investors (and the operative word here is "consistently") do have a different way of thinking. They are so often ahead of the crowd because they stay informed and have the courage and the confidence to take action.

THE TEN COMMANDMENTS

So how can you join this exclusive group? Well, there's no password or secret handshake to master. All you have to do is learn the basic principles, the Ten Commandments I mentioned in the introduction, and get started.

1. What?

You have an entire investment spectrum spread out in front of you. There are single-family homes, condos, commercial properties, hotels, raw land, and all the sub-categories and combinations thereof. You have to make a choice, and to do that you have to ask some questions about yourself. How much skill and experience do I have? How much time do I have to devote to this? How much risk can I entertain? How much money do I have, and what size investment can I handle? What is my timeline — long term, short term? After you've fleshed out this picture, take those categories of investments that have not been eliminated, put them in order of preference, and then go looking. In this, as in everything else, you have to have an idea of what you're after. Then you have to make a choice and take action. We're going to keep coming back to this theme time and time again.

2. Where?

Once again, you're faced with an embarrassment of choices. Downtown is close; our own suburb is closer. What about neighbouring municipalities and small towns? Do I go out of province? What about out of the country? Conventional wisdom says that the closer you are to what you buy, the happier you are going to be. But this is not always the case.

There are times when the best investment available is thousands of kilometres away. You have to take each situation on a case-by-case basis and make your decision on the factors existing at the time. In other words, scrutinize the options, make a choice, then go looking for opportunities.

3. When?

There's no such thing as a bad piece of real estate, but there is real estate that you can buy too early or too late. Timing is everything. Back in the days of runaway inflation, the calendar would bail you out if you bought too soon. But those days are gone. Today, it will cost you if you buy too soon. And remember that any money you waste on the purchase price is profit that could have been yours when you sell.

Timing has to be considered within the framework of other factors, of course — especially real estate trends. If the trend is moving towards a particular category of real estate in a particular area, you may find it more difficult to buy at the price and terms that fit your formula. Perhaps you will have to wait until trends change or a unique opportunity appears. But be vigilant — if a good deal surfaces at a price you're willing to pay, then there's always someone else who's also willing to pay it. You've got to be decisive and you've got to be quick — but you also have to be right.

4. Why?

You don't buy something just because you believe you'll make X amount of dollars on it. It has to fit within the framework of your investment objectives. The risk factors have to be in balance with what you can tolerate, and everything has to be considered in light of any economic, sociological, and demographic factors that may apply. But the only way you're going to be able to evaluate all this is by doing your own due diligence. (We'll see some examples of the traps due diligence can reveal in Commandment 8, "What to Watch For.") This is one of the points at which you will make or lose the most money. It's like panning for gold — the trick is to get rid of the sand without washing away the gold itself.

When you're considering a new property, pay special attention to the "why" questions. Why is the vendor so anxious to sell? Why has this property been listed for three weeks with no offers? Why hasn't anyone else thought of turning this storefront into a restaurant? I like to advise people to buy a piece of property only when they get enough yes answers to the questions they ask. But remember: You will prosper or suffer in direct relation to the number of correct questions you ask.

5. How Much?

Remember that the price you pay is not just the dollar figure — it is a combination of the dollar figure and the financing terms. You could pay twice the price of an apartment building, for example, if you bought it for nothing down and paid off the mortgage at no interest plus half the net operating profit.

The conventional wisdom used to be that the route to financial freedom was to buy a property, hold it as the appreciation mounted, and then sell it to realize the profit from the inflation. In an inflationary environment that's fine, but if the inflation graph is a flat line, your profit is going to be contained in the price you paid (in other words, you have to find a bargain). As an investor, you must first determine the current fair market value — and then buy below that value. With taxes, real estate commissions, closing costs, etc., you must pay at least 12 percent less than the current market value if you want to sell the next day and just break even. So obviously buying at the right price is crucial.

And don't be afraid to offer the price *you* want to pay. You can buy anything that's out there, remember, but the seller usually has just this one property for sale. You know in advance that his asking price represents his absolute wildest dream. You'll be amazed what sellers will say yes to.

6. How?

How will you finance the deal? What kind of terms can you arrange? Which bankers, lawyers, agents, and accountants will you use to finalize the deal? These are all the kinds of questions you will have to ask yourself when you are ready to make a purchase.

This is where technique comes in, the nuts and bolts of getting from point A (looking) to point B (buying). This is where the buyer with twenty years' experience should have an advantage over the person with one year. Yet often we see experienced investors making the same mistakes over and over. You don't want to be one of those people who is still a beginner after twenty years in the business.

The way to avoid this is to learn from any mistakes you make — and even better, to learn from the mistakes other people make. That is why the most successful investors are the ones who are perpetual students.

7. How Long?

How long should you hold on to a property? This is different for everyone. It depends on the external forces of the marketplace and the internal forces of your own motivations and objectives. Are you a keeper or a flipper? Fortunes have been made with both approaches.

When you wake up each morning, you should consider each property you own and how much you could sell it for that day. Then ask yourself this question: If I didn't own this property but it was for sale and I had the money, would I buy it for its current market value? If the answer is yes, you should keep that property another day. If the answer is no, you should put that property on the market. In effect, every day that you don't attempt to sell a piece of property for its fair market value, you are repurchasing it for that amount. Every day. No exceptions.

Of course, a lot of people buy and never sell. Now, if you started with a few million and never had to look at a property again after buying, this would work just fine for you. But most other people (those who want to get the million) want to optimize their results, and for them the examination-and-evaluation procedure is a constant process. These people would do well to learn that nothing ever stays the same. As I've already said, the only constant is change. Whether you're a flipper or a keeper, the closer you watch the market, the better off you're going to be.

8. What to Watch For

Everything! The marketplace is full of quicksand, and if you don't do the necessary due diligence, you will eventually make a serious and expensive mistake. But be forewarned: the greatest dangers lie not with the property itself, but with the people you encounter and external situations that can impact on your property.

Sellers will tell you only what suits their purposes. Sure, there are laws, but laws don't cover everything. Believe it or not, it is possible to buy land and then find that, under certain circumstances, you don't have access to it. As many innocent property owners in British Columbia and Ontario found, for example, there are lots where the roads leading in cross First Nations' land that the Natives can close anytime they want. There are also properties with restrictive covenants in favour of hydro utilities or railways. Or imagine your conundrum if you bought a piece of commercial property that had been a gas station for forty years and had ground so contaminated that it could take five years to clean it up enough to get a development permit. The examples could go on forever.

You might not have known about any restrictions when you bought the property — or perhaps you knew about them but didn't realize their importance — yet if the buyer you're trying to sell to wants the title free and clear, you won't be able to deliver.

The point is that you can avoid a danger only before you buy. After you buy, it's too late.

9. Who to Trust

Most people are not going to make a full-time career out of real estate investing, so they are not going to become expert in the myriad areas where expertise is required. Therefore, they are going to have to rely on some outside experts. Indeed, even the full-time practitioners have to turn to specialists when they come to areas where they don't have the knowledge they need.

Choosing lawyers, accountants, and insurance agents — in other words, people whom you are using for implementation — is a relatively simple process. But selecting people to help you make value judgements is a much more complex and absolutely critical process. This is another place where you make or lose a lot of money. Ask any real estate investors — or for that matter, any investors of any kind — and they will all tell you the same thing. They made the most money when they did their own due diligence; when they lost money, it was because they listened to the wrong people.

Track record is an indicator, but it's not enough by itself. You have to know how much an adviser is getting paid and by whom. You have to know if his objectives are close enough to yours so that your trust will be well placed.

10. If?

One of my mentors from my early years in the business told me, "All the money I've made in real estate, I've made by saying yes. All the money I've kept, I've kept by saying no." After you've gone through the process of asking the foregoing nine questions, you must take all the answers and examine them to gain an answer to the tenth question: If I buy this property, what kind of profit can I expect over what period of time?

If your profit is in doubt, say no. Opportunities are like streetcars — there's another one coming along in ten minutes. As long as you're in the marketplace, you're going to have more opportunities than you will have time, money, or energy.

So be cautious, but not too cautious. Remember: you can't get results without action!

◈

In Essence

◇ Ask as many questions as you can think of. It's not the things you don't know that kill you — it's those things you assume to be true that aren't.

◇ Do your own due diligence. If you don't, you will pay not only for the mistakes you make, but also for the mistakes you allow other people to make.

◇ Be patient. Opportunities come along in a constant stream.

◇ Once you've made the decision to act, don't delay. Nothing happens until you take action.

2

Timing

Reporter: I understand you're a very successful comedian.
Entertainer: Yes, I am.
Reporter: What is the secret of your succ —
Entertainer: Timing!

In stand-up comedy and practically everything else in life, timing is everything. In real estate investing, the degree to which your timing is accurate is the degree to which you will achieve results. In fact, timing is very often the difference between success and failure. Perhaps that's true, you may well be saying, but — and I hear this all the time — what about location, location, location? Everybody trots out this principle as the guiding light to successful real estate investing. Poppycock. To my mind, this is actually the worst cliché in the marketplace today.

Developers, realtors, and reporters repeat those three words *ad nauseum*, yet they really have nothing to do with value appreciation. Sure, some locations are better than others — a lot in Toronto is worth more than a lot in Saskatoon, for example — but in any given market, it is far more important for the average investor (or the average homeowner, for that matter) to understand the principle of timing.

To illustrate this, let's consider a suburb in Vancouver, say Burnaby. If you had bought an average bungalow in any location in that fair suburb in 1989, you would have paid about $260,000 for it. Let's say you ran it into the ground, didn't cut the grass, and sold it to me in 1995. I would have paid the then prevailing value of $400,000, and you would have made a hefty profit. To continue this illustration, let's assume I cleaned up the house, finished the basement, and cut the grass diligently. Yet when I want to sell the house in 1999, it's worth only $350,000. I lost and you gained — same location.

Had you bought a house in Toronto — in any location — the scenario would have been the same. If you bought in 1985 and sold in 1989, you were a hero. But if you bought the same house in the same location at the peak in 1989, you were a bum. I could tell you the same story about New York, San Diego, Los Angeles, Phoenix, Calgary, Hong Kong, Tokyo, Berlin, and so on and so on. Whatever area you live in, check your marketplace. You will find the same principle at work there. So what should this tell you? Forget about location, location, location and start to think about timing! Where is the real estate market cycle in my area? What influences the cycle? What are the principles? Remember that real estate markets are always local, never national, and so are the cycles.

WHAT MAKES TIMING SO IMPORTANT?

So you say, "Good! I will learn what I have to learn about timing, and then I will know how to invest. Where do I start? What are the rules?" Well, opportunities used to be easier to identify in the past. Timing wasn't as important then because the dynamics seldom changed, but today's dynamics change constantly. In the new millennium, we are more likely to move into small towns, have greater population flows, see new job creation at home, and experience a hundred other factors that may affect value. We expect these changes to increase in velocity. Just when you think you have it figured out, the rules change.

Let's say, for example, that I take you onto the tennis court to teach you the game. I hit the ball to you with a certain amount of force and it travels from my racquet in a straight direction on a certain trajectory at a relatively constant speed. Easy enough. You have normal eye/hand coordination and normal motor skills, so if we practise this for a while you will learn the timing involved.

But when you go out to play competitive tennis with someone else, you find yourself in a game where the ball angles left or right in mid-flight. The trajectory unexpectedly goes up or down. The speed of the ball changes without warning. Suddenly, the timing you learned when you were being taught the game is of little or no use. In fact, to add insult to injury, you find yourself running to where the ball is not going to be.

Real estate investment is like that surreal tennis game. When you look at the market, you are looking at a snapshot in time. That's the way it is at that moment, but it may be very different in a month or a year. As with tennis, you have to adjust for the conditions of the "game" and try to anticipate where the "ball" will go based on those conditions.

Now, if you are in an inflationary real estate cycle, anticipating where the ball is going to go is relatively simple. You buy a piece of property using leverage, wait a certain amount of time for the property to appreciate, then sell for a profit or borrow on your increased equity and buy something in addition. What could be easier?

Even if you're in a flat-line segment of an inflation cycle, the rules of the game are clear. You have to buy below fair market value to establish your profit at the beginning. You have to give greater importance to cash flow.

Both scenarios seem clear. But what happens if you buy in an inflationary cycle and then it turns flat? You have to learn to shift your focus every time the market changes. Read the changes, interpret what they mean, and adapt yourself to them.

DETERMINING THE DETERMINING FACTORS

So which particular factors have the most influence on the market value of property? Well, there are several, including (as we've already seen) inflation. But the good news is that these factors, called determining factors, are not especially complex or difficult to deal with. Still, each factor does have a bearing on all the others, and all of them affect the price of property and thus the timing.

Let's look at the six most common determining factors in a little more detail. (These aren't in order of importance, but they are all important in the order of things. Taken together, they will give you a clearer picture of how to determine the timing of your real estate investment.)

Migration

If you're looking for prices to go up, any migration has to be an inward migration. After all, what is it that makes the price of real estate go up? Demand.

Usually, any population increase equals the increase in the price of real estate. The determining factor is not just the number of people, however; it is the number of people and the size of the area into which they move. If you move a thousand people into a thousand square kilometres, for example, you have a density increase of one person per square kilometre. But if you move a thousand people into ten square kilometres, your density increase is a hundred times more and will have a much greater impact on the prices.

For any in-migration to occur, there have to be economic or sociological factors that attract people. In the 1930s, Las Vegas was a wide spot in the road where you stopped for gas. You could have bought the whole town for practically nothing. But today, thanks to the casinos, you'll find some of the most expensive real estate in the world there. Still, if you go ten miles into the desert, you can buy all the land you want for a few hundred dollars an acre. Will that land ever be worth what the land in downtown Las Vegas is worth? Not likely. Who wants to go there?

When you see a marked increase in inward migration, you know that the timing is probably right for purchasing. But it matters greatly why people are coming. If the government built a new dam and created a lake, that lake is going to be there for a long time. Good place to buy. However, if somebody built a Hula Hoop factory, it's likely that the factory will shut down when the fad is over. Probably not a good place to buy. In Porcupine Plain or Shell Lake, Saskatchewan, you can buy a building lot for one dollar. The catch is that you have to live there. In any major metropolitan centre, by contrast, a waterfront lot is priced at a million dollars or more. Of course, everyone wants to live there. This is the only time when location matters.

So where can you go to get an idea of migratory trends? Your Statistics Canada office and federal and provincial departments of immigration all publish the relevant numbers. In fact, StatsCan ranks winners by city and projects future trends. Get the numbers over time and you'll have an idea of your area's prospects.

Affordability

Beyond air to breathe, there isn't anything more important than shelter. But that shelter has to be affordable. If property in an area costs less than comparable properties in comparable areas but there's a demand for it, it's probably time for its price to rise. If property is selling for less than its replacement cost, it's probably time for its price to rise. If property values are equal to replacement costs and there are no vacancies, it's probably time to build.

Value is always an important consideration, but affordability is much more important. Let's say, for example, that you buy an apartment complex. Your tenants have to be able to afford your rents or they will go someplace else. In other words, what you buy not only has to have value on its own, but also has to be affordable to the end user.

So how do you gauge affordability? Well, many federal agencies publish affordability ratings, as do all major banks. In 1995, the Canada Mortgage and Housing Corp. (CMHC) ranked, by house price, all major North American cities, from the least affordable to the most affordable. Vancouver came in third, after Honolulu and San Francisco. Toronto was twenty-third and Calgary forty-seventh. Needless to say, an affordability rating isn't the only number to look at, but when looked at in conjunction with other factors, it may help you pick a city.

Inventory Availability

Here's where the law of supply and demand kicks in. If there are too many of a certain type of property available in a particular price range, then prices are more likely to decrease than increase. By contrast, if supply is low but demand is high, prices will surely rise.

There is also a relationship between inventory availability and affordability. When affordability becomes a problem, people will compress downwards. Instead of a house, they'll settle for a condo or an apartment. Instead of a three-bedroom, they'll settle for a two-bedroom and use the den as a sleeping area, if need be. When this happens, more expensive accommodations stagnate.

So be sure to watch the statistics on available inventory. Local real estate boards and major brokerage firms all publish the relevant monthly and yearly numbers. Some boards even publish running totals of five years or more. When you see those numbers start to move in either direction, act accordingly.

Inflation

Inflation comes and goes. Every time it rises, up spring three schools of thought: the "it'll go up forever" school; the "it's going to stay where it is now" school; and the "we're in for some deflation" school. The same thing happens every time it declines.

The truth, of course, is that no one knows what will happen next; no one has a crystal ball. The world has changed and is continuing to change. The U.S. stock market crashed by 40 percent in 1974 and by 28 percent in 1987, and gloom descended on real estate markets in sympathy. But by the late 1990s, the Dow Jones seemed to hit a new record high almost every day. In 1981-82 in Canada and 1988-92 in the U.S., real estate values crashed and mortgage rates hit 16.5 percent. Throughout this turmoil, there were those predicting a return to inflation and those predicting an absolute crash into deflation. Yet had you listened to all the doom and gloom of 1961, 1974, 1981, 1982, 1983, 1986, and 1988 and not bought real estate, you would have done yourself a serious disservice. If you are banking on deflation, the odds aren't with you. Inflation has returned time and again.

Environment of Growth

This is the toughest determining factor to read because here we are dealing much more with the headlines on the front page than the statistics in the business section. In essence, this involves predicting the future growth potential of an area.

Are people coming in because there are jobs? Is industry making major investments? Is this a one-industry town? Will the new highway add to this area or will it bypass the town, condemning businesses to die? Is the local government relatively easy to get along with? Is the federal government reasonable with taxation? Do management and labour manage to get along? Can an investor expect a fair return for the capital invested? These are just some of the factors that contribute to an environment of growth. If times are good, that's good. But there can be even more potential in bad times that are starting to get better.

When he was teaching me to play soccer, my coach told me I had to know only one thing and that was to run to the ball. "Wherever the ball is," he used to say, "you run to it!" With real estate investment, you run to the environment of growth. And always remember to watch for changes. It is the changes that tell you when the time is getting right to either buy or sell.

Demographics

The buzzword of today is demographics. During the Second World War, when a lot of able-bodied men were away in the army, the maternity wards weren't very busy. When the war was over, everybody made up for lost time. The result was the baby boom of the late 1940s. As these boomers move through life, the demographic bulge they create sparks very important changes in the marketplace. All of a sudden, for example, joggers and tennis players and aerobicizers become golfers. In a few more years, those golfers will become lawn bowlers and mall walkers.

So how does all this apply to real estate? Well, not surprisingly, there are two schools of thought. One school says that the baby boomers have already bought their single-family homes, and that as they die off, so will the need for single-family detached housing. A similar scenario holds that as their kids grow up and leave home, the boomers will want to divest themselves of that house in the city and go someplace less urban and more pleasant. Either scenario would mean that fewer housing starts would be required. Instead, there would be a glut of houses on the market at the same time, creating more supply than demand.

Now, the other school of thought says something rather different. It theorizes that many boomers are going to be active later in life and stay in their homes longer. No old-age home for them. Besides, the kids who leave home at nineteen now come back at twenty-two. Then they come back again with two kids of their own when they get divorced. So there isn't going to be a shortage of bodies to fill those extra bedrooms.

Which one of these schools of thought is right? Maybe both, or maybe neither. It doesn't ultimately matter, because demographic forecasts are primarily for long-range projections. To individual businesses working in the day-to-day world, they rank way down on the list of important considerations. Business is concerned with economics (the general local business environment), operating practices (how to successfully compete in the market), sales and marketing (how to service customers), and then, maybe, demographics. The same is true of real estate investors. For them, local conditions always override long-term projections. Although demographic forecasts may have an important role to play, they should be considered only within the context of all the other determining factors I've identified.

THE IMPORTANCE OF BEING CONTRARY

So how does the average person learn to read these determining factors? Believe it or not, one of the shortcuts is to take the contrarian view, the stance that the public is always wrong. This flies in the face of logic, but it's true. The public *is* always wrong. Let's go back to Las Vegas to see this in action. You have a piece of land that has been worth practically nothing since the dawn of history because nobody wants it. Suddenly, there is a demand for that land, prices start to go up, and everybody wants to jump on the bandwagon. They say, "Hey, now is the time to buy," but they're wrong. This is the time to *sell*. The time to buy was back when prices first started to go up.

It always amazes me that at peak market cycles, the press proclaims things have never been better and they will get better yet. But at the bottom, they have never been worse and will always get worse yet. For some reason, we believe that if six buyers wrestle each other to the ground in the living room of a listed home and one emerges victorious, paying $20,000 more than the place is worth at a 12 percent interest rate, it is a good market. When the buyer can save the $20,000 and pay only 6 percent interest, however, it becomes a terrible market. Same place, same city, same property — yet somehow worse.

The fact is that markets rise with demand until they get overheated, fall until demand is dead, and then rise again to complete another cycle. So how is someone supposed to know when changes are coming? You can read the beginning of changes in statistics. Now, usually the change has already occurred by the time you see a report forecasting that change is coming. What you have to do is go directly to the source of the numbers — those various boards, bureaus, and agencies — and get the news while it's still news. If you're Internet literate, you can go right to the World Wide Web and be in at the beginning. Or you can get an unbiased "real estate only" newsletter and fax publisher to do it for you (wink, wink, nudge, nudge).

Is it possible to predict the length of a trend? Well, not exactly, but historically real estate cycles go in four-year swings. A single swing is from peak to peak or from valley to valley. It's interesting to note that we find this four-year cycle repeated in other situations. For example, you should always try to time your mortgage to come due during a U.S. presidential election year, because — like magic — the interest rates will always be lowest in those years.

THE LAST WORD

Once you study the statistical factors and the numbers involved, you'll be able to apply a stop-loss factor to your real estate investments. You should apply the principle to your real estate dealings much as you would if you were trading in commodities or stocks. Naturally, you want to let your profits run as long as they are going forward, but if things start to change, you want to limit the retrogression as much as possible.

A good way to do this is to watch the inflation rate. Historically, house prices have always risen on par with or slightly ahead of the inflation rate. So your profit rate will generally be tied to the inflation rate. However, during the late 1980s and early 1990s governments around the world, particularly in North America, changed how they calculated the inflation rate. In the United States, for example, tax increases and house-price increases, both new and old, were taken out of the index. In Canada, only new home prices are now a factor. As a result, from the late 1990s on, there has been a greater margin of error in trying to read indicators for the purpose of predicting trends. You can run into some misleading factors.

In 1998, for example, real estate values were rising by more than 9 percent per annum throughout the United States while the official rate of inflation was 1.5 percent. Calgary's home prices rose by 13 percent and Toronto's by 7 percent. Yet we had an official inflation rate of 0.5 percent. In other words, we can't compare these unadjusted factors in a straight line. That means it will pay to keep an eye on these indices — as long as you are comparing apples with apples.

There are signposts from outside the real estate arena too, of course. You have to be aware of what's happening politically and economically, on both a broad and local scale. Remember that change never happens in a vacuum — everything impacts on everything else. The more information you have, the more likely you are to make the right decision.

Nevertheless, it's not necessary for you to have the wisdom of the entire world at your fingertips. You need not master the intricacies of economics to be able to predict if ageing baby boomers will be concerned about their retirement funds. You don't need to understand whether this retirement money is going to exert a downward pressure on interest rates, therefore making cheaper money available (which in turn facilitates the development and purchase of new housing).

This should all interest you, but it isn't necessary for you to be able to predict it. When it happens, you'll read about it in the paper while you drink your morning coffee. What you should really be focused on is anything taking place in the specific segment of the marketplace where you are concentrating your attention. Think of the real estate arena as a giant stock market. You don't buy every stock that's on the board. Instead, you select a category, and from that category you pick a few stocks. These are the ones you watch. In real estate, you decide on your categories — detached houses, condos, apartments, urban, rural, etc. — then keep a close eye on those you've chosen and regard the rest with only a general interest (so you'll know if and when it's prudent to switch categories).

The bottom line is that you have to be able to read the changes or find someone to read them for you. And always be ready to act!

In Essence

◇ We have to read changes, interpret their meaning, and then adapt to them.
› The public is always wrong.
› Demand makes real estate increase in price.
› You don't have to know it all — knowing enough about your specialty will make you rich.

3

Trends

Change is the only constant.

I t used to be so simple. All you had to do was buy a piece of property in a good location, keep breathing in and out for a period of time, sell it for a big profit, and then do it all over again. But if you try to do that in today's low-inflation market, you can make some very serious mistakes. Now you have to watch the trends, and the direction of those trends will tell you where your money should be invested (or not invested, as the case may be).

I once asked one of my mentors to explain the difference between a danger and a risk. His answer was illuminating. He said, "A risk is a negative variable that *may* occur. Once it *has* occurred, it becomes a danger." Careful observation of real estate trends will very often pinpoint the negatives before they occur, thus allowing us to avoid them. I can hear your first question now: What are real estate trends? Well, a trend is a change in any factor that has an effect on the price of real estate.

For instance, if you had wanted to invest in Surrey, B.C., in 1992, it would have been far more important for you to understand both timing and trends than to robotically chant the "location, location, location" mantra. The "location" espousers actually knocked Surrey — it was not the recommended place to be — and touted the wall of new condos going up on Vancouver's waterfront. But between 1986 and 1991, the city of Surrey grew by more than 68,000 people. This was more growth than was experienced by all of the Atlantic and Prairie provinces (excluding Alberta) combined. Had you bought a building lot anywhere in much-maligned Surrey, you would have been up by some 150 percent (the average lot price soared from $55,000 to $160,000 in just four years). Meanwhile, those must-have Vancouver condos had dropped in value by 15 percent or more by 1995. The huge inward migration drove values — locations be damned. Most investors made a fatal mistake in believing that this migration to the "wrong" location didn't matter; the trend was huge, and values followed.

SOME COMMON MYTHS

To determine if a trend is really likely to have an impact on real estate prices, you should constantly ask yourself the following questions:

- What is the trend, and does it matter to real estate investors?
- Is this trend real?
- Which way is the trend going?
- Is it likely to continue in that direction?
- How far will it go?
- How long will it last?

It doesn't matter whether you gather this data yourself or rely on an expert, so long as you ask the questions and get the answers. But don't do this just once and then forget about it. You have to ask these questions over and over — about every determining factor, every category, and every piece of real estate that you look at from now until you're too myopic to look any more.

While you're gathering all this information, be careful to separate trends that have an impact on price from those that don't. There are many common myths about real estate price appreciation. The "location, location, location" myth is just one. We have dozens of others, and here are some of the most prevalent.

Interest Rates Drive Markets Higher

You see this announced everywhere. For some reason, the media project stronger real estate prices because of lower interest rates. Yet history shows that while low interest rates do impact on affordability — that is, you can buy higher-priced homes at lower mortgage rates — they have nothing whatever to do with price appreciation. In 1979, the average house price in Vancouver was $78,000. By May 1981, that had soared to $180,000. Yet at the very same time, five-year mortgage rates climbed from 9.75 percent to more than 16.5 percent. Since 1995, interest rates have been reduced a total of thirty-six times and are now at a forty-four-year record low of 6 percent for a five-year term. Yet housing prices fell from an average price of $345,000 in February 1995 to approximately $280,000 by the end of 1998.

Interest rates do *not* determine value. What drove prices up in 1981 was the perception of investors and homeowners that things would always go higher. "High interest rates be damned," they said. "I don't mind paying 15 percent if I make $50,000 profit." Yet at other times, even times of record lows, they said, "I won't buy."

So instead of blithely accepting that prices go higher because of low rates, you should study their real impact. They do tend to mean, for example, that buyers who would normally have held off for a couple of years before making the plunge are motivated to move into the market. But be aware that there can be only so many bites on the carcass. If these buyers come into the market earlier, that means they're not there to come in later.

And interestingly, values actually tend to climb when rates begin to rise. This is because many buyers who were previously sitting on the fence jump in, worried they might miss the bandwagon. However, if interest rates rise too far (as was the case in 1981) the engine of interest rates/affordability will indeed sputter and die.

All Foreign Immigration Is Good for Real Estate

It isn't enough to know that there is immigration — you also need to know what kind of immigration there is. If you are looking for price appreciation in an upscale area, for instance, strong refugee immigration doesn't help much. Be sure to break down immigration statistics into their base components. Entrepreneur-class immigrants bring money and generally create businesses and jobs, while refugees often need more of a helping hand in the form of federal subsidies.

SOME PRESUMPTIONS ARE CORRECT

Of course, none of what I've just said means that there aren't any commonly held beliefs that are true. Here are some of the ones I think are most important.

Inward Migration Does Matter

Yes, I know we already discussed this under timing. But I think this is a significant enough trend that it merits further consideration. Why is inward migration so important? Well, the people already living in an area have a place to sleep and a place to work and facilities for entertaining themselves for the other eight hours a day. But new people coming in need all those amenities, and that in-migration is going to have an effect. From 1986 to 1991, for example, Vancouver's population grew by 16.5 percent, or more than double the national average. From then until 1997, it grew by more than 2.5 percent per year. People wanted — for whatever reason — to be in Vancouver. (The reasons for this in-migration are not all that important to you as a real estate investor. Nevertheless, you may want to uncover these reasons so you can keep an eye on them and get ahead of the game.) Even with falling population rates, Vancouver will probably have added more than a million souls to its roster by the year 2020. This is a very strong engine indeed, for these new arrivals bring in fresh hopes, skills, and money — all of which drive up existing housing prices.

Migration, both in and out, is a factor that has to be watched. But remember that every community has its own individual growth rate. Find out both the actual and the projected growth rate for the area in which you wish to invest before making a move.

How to Identify Inward Migration Trends

Every community in Canada is surveyed every five years, and you can get population statistics from StatsCan, Immigration Canada, or the CMHC office in your area. Look at the quantity and quality of immigrants from offshore, as well as at interprovincial migration numbers.

There are other yardsticks too. A friend of mine who is a very astute real estate investor said that there was a time when you could gauge an exodus or an influx just by counting U-Haul trailers. His recommendation was to go to the highway and note the number and direction of all U-Haul trailers. If they were coming into town, good times were on the way. If they were heading out of town, that was a storm warning.

I've always felt that this was an ingenious barometer of what was going on. I'm sure that somewhere in the government there is a department with hundreds of employees all devoted to gathering information that could have been obtained by sending one person out to the highway. But that's a whole different crusade.

Supply and Demand Make a Difference

Supply and demand do not exist in a vacuum — they are interrelated. But they also vary from time to time and place to place. Things can be completely different from one province to the next — or even from one block to the next. You can have single-family homes, townhouses, condos, and rental apartments all in the same stretch, and the supply and demand will be completely different for each one.

But the basics don't change. If there are more buyers than sellers, clearly there will be upward price pressures. If there are more sellers than buyers, there will be downward price pressures. Prices will adjust to reflect the number of units on the market and the number of buyers. It always has been this way and it will always continue to be this way. You do, however, have to continue watching for changes in trends so you'll know whether to be a buyer or a seller. And even if you have identified a trend such as population growth correctly, you still have to watch the supply side. Astute builders and developers watch the same statistics as you. In a competitive world, their rush to capitalize may push you to an early financial grave.

Let's look at Whistler, B.C., for an example of this. Even though the town's population growth was high, our newsletter team decided to place Whistler on investor alert in February 1997. If you ever want to be intensely disliked, put a ski resort on investor alert. Don't we realize that it is a great mountain? Indeed. Isn't the population going to keep on increasing? Probably. Hasn't Whistler been rated the number-one resort in North America? Absolutely. But although the population trend said buy, we felt the supply-and-demand trend screamed sell. The condo and condo-hotel building boom was, in our opinion, outstripping any sane population/ski visitors/tourist growth increases by a wide margin. Thus, investor alert.

Oh, and by the way, we were right. Whistler values crashed *after* our warning.

The Changing Workplace

The world is changing, and old, monolithic big business has to move over. StatsCan reports that 81 percent of all new job growth comes in companies with fewer than twenty employees. Whether they like it or not, the big companies are having to make room for all those small, flexible, export-hungry new firms. I call these the mongoose businesses. (The mongoose always beats the cobra because his reflexes are so fast and his reaction time is so quick that, for him, the cobra seems to be moving in slow motion.)

As technology develops, our lifestyle choices multiply. The fax machine, the computer, the satellite dish, and the cellphone have given everyone seven-league boots. Physical locale has become much less relevant in business. Those who want to are going to be able to relocate to small towns and outlying areas. This footloose worker is a brand-new engine indeed, so we will watch him to see where he goes and what he does when he gets there. Yet another trend that will tell us what to buy and where to buy it.

WHAT WILL THE FUTURE HOLD?

Today's real estate investor, if he wants optimal results, keeps a close and continual watch on all of these trends. Any one of them has the power to lift prices up or push them down. And of course, there are numerous possible combinations and permutations, which will become maxi-trends or mini-trends depending on how they affect the market.

You want to watch the trends because they will tell you what to buy, when to buy, and where to buy. That's how you're going to make money. But you also want to know when it's time to run for the hills. That's how you get to keep the money after you make it.

So now we've looked at some of the conventional trends, including inward migration, affordability, supply and demand, and inflation. But there are also some new trends to consider. I will expand on all of these in the chapters that follow, but here's a taste of what's to come.

New Government

When it looks like governments are going to change, this could herald a new trend in real estate. Ontario and Alberta were basket cases in 1993. In 1999, they were thriving. B.C. was a booming province in 1992; in 1998, it struggled.

Out with Government

Given our continued disenchantment with all things political, we will continue to force government to downsize. Knowing this, our newsletter team was quick to place Ottawa and several provincial capitals on investor alert. In fact, investors should be wary of any community totally dependent on government services. The only exceptions are communities that administer large outside amounts of cash. Any city entrusted with overseeing a Native land-claim settlement, for example, is a safer bet.

The Superstore Index

A few years ago, some students at the University of Cologne came up with an ingenious way to predict the strength of worldwide economies. They called it the Big Mac index. Using the price of a Big Mac, they could fairly accurately calculate the strength of a number of national economies. If the sandwich cost $2.95 in Berlin, $9.00 in Hong Kong, and $3.15 in Toronto, the conclusion was clear. The Big Mac of real estate might be called the superstore index. Whenever a Costco, Price Club, Wal-Mart, or other superstore opens in a given location, it stands to reason that the future growth of the community will be strong. These stores open only in communities that their research (they have more money than you do for research) shows will thrive. Where they go, active families live and will continue to live.

Where They Play, Real Estate Will Stay

In many places in Canada, gambling is now a fact of life. Although I am not particularly fond of them, casinos — at least first-class ones — can add value to markets. They attract new employees, new visitors. House prices in Windsor and the whole Niagara Peninsula rose in value by more than 20 percent when casinos opened there.

The Great Move Out of Town

Some small towns are growing at four to five times the national average. Investing in small towns, however, is an art form unto itself. They can provide terrific opportunities, but sometimes, because of their size, they can also be frighteningly volatile. In a "single industry" town, for instance, a plant closing can have a drastic effect. Strikes in that industry can devastate the economy. Military towns can similarly be killed when a base shuts down. (I'll explain this in more detail in chapter 21.)

Resort Buying

With their new-found wealth, many people can now buy that second vacation home or even future residences in special resorts. But generally speaking, you should not expect to profit if all you have is a chairlift and a parking lot. The second-home buyer will pick style, class, and ambience over roughing it every time. It is more important with this type of real estate than any other to understand the different investment classes offered.

Restrictions in Industrial Zoning

If you own a property zoned for heavy industry, hang on to it. No municipality will grant new zoning for the environmentally unfriendly heavy user. As companies downsize and diversify, all industrial property will benefit, especially those near highways and rail lines (yes, here location does make a difference).

Downsized Families Mean New Storage Needs

Mini-storage parks will be money-makers. Their benefits include huge cash flow and minimal overhead (deluxe storage means you provide a light bulb to illuminate the four concrete walls), and they're a real estate play to boot (because there's always the potential for a higher and better use of the land).

New Jobs for a New World

In the future, you will make money on information in only two ways: by originating it or interpreting it. This will create the need for new professions: joint-venture specialists, troubled-property specialists, mortgage brokers, resort-only professional property managers. Specialists will reign. The home-renovation business in Canada will surpass all new construction within six years (it already has in the Atlantic provinces).

Technology

Technology changes our lives every day in a million little (and not so little) ways. But on the real estate side of things, we're seeing only the tip of the iceberg. With computers continuing to drop in price, everyone will soon be able to afford one. The proliferation of information will be astounding, and the ramifications for the real estate industry are enormous.

Already real estate brokers have downsized by an average of more than 40 percent in eight years. Sales commissions will crash, and what income is left will shift to the selling agent from the listing agent. Appraisers will disappear, to be replaced by computerized programs. Dozens of current professions will have to change dramatically or will disappear altogether. "Adjust or die" will be the battle-cry of the day. But of course, for the astute investor this means untold opportunities to find new deals and new buyers in places that were out of reach in the past.

THE LAST WORD

So what have we learned from this crash course in trend analysis? Above all, we've learned that when you identify a trend and want to buy into it, you should shop the market and bargain hard. If it's not the deal of a lifetime, go on to the next one. A super-abundance of sellers and a shortage of buyers is bad news for the sellers. As Sancho Panza said to Don Quixote, "If the stone hits the bottle or the bottle hits the stone, it's going to be bad for the bottle."

Trends will tell you what to do and when to do it. For optimum results, you have to become at least a student (and hopefully a master) of those trends.

In Essence

> There are true trends and there are myths.
> Trends are cyclical, and the investor has to keep watching to know what to do.
> The basics don't change. If there are more buyers than sellers, the price will go up.
> Today's market is more complex and the people in it more knowledgeable. You have to keep up or you'll get left behind.
> Technology will become the key to unlocking real estate riches.

4

The Small Investor vs. the Large Investor

Let me tell you about the very rich. They are different from you and me.

— *F. Scott Fitzgerald*

Yes, they have more money.

— *Ernest Hemingway*

Large investors and small investors have some similarities and many differences. No matter which type you are, it's important that you know how to thrive and even more important that you know how to survive. Almost all small investors want to grow to be large investors. Almost none of the large investors want to become small investors.

Most people reading this book are going to be small investors — and of course, there are more small deals than there arc big deals — so, of necessity, we will turn our attention more in that direction. But it is important to stress that when I talk about "small" and "large" investors, I am referring not just to the size of the deal but also to investment objectives. The small investor and the large investor sometimes differ greatly in their objectives.

GETTING THE FIRST OLIVE OUT OF THE BOTTLE

The first problem for the small investor is getting enough money for that initial deal. I like to call this getting the first olive out of the bottle — and it can be tough. This is why so many small investors fall prey to scams.

Damon Runyon once wrote, "The race is not always to the swift, nor the battle to the strong — however, that's the way to bet." And that's also the way it is with real estate scams and small investors (I talk about scams in more detail in chapter 13). The scammers almost never get sent to jail, so after a time they become proficient at their craft. But the small investor gets wiped out and has to start all over again.

Unfortunately, scam investments are seductively attractive to the small investor because they allow him to participate in a market he has long coveted. For his whole life, he's had pounded into him the idea that real estate will keep him warm and safe, so he had better get some. He, like everyone else, has that friend or brother-in-law who is always bragging about all his wonderful deals. And so our small investor can hardly wait to dive into those shark-infested waters — and sadly, sometimes he has to be bitten several times before the sharks become a reality for him.

Of course, once he has dived in, he finds the market to be daunting. And because he usually doesn't have enough money to invest alone, he opts to join up with a professional management group. All too often, this is where he makes a fatal mistake. Almost before he can even blink, there goes whatever little capital he had and he's out of the game. So here's our first rule of small investing: don't give your money to a person (or group of people) who is going to lose it.

Sounds self-evident, doesn't it? Well, you'd be surprised. At the time of this writing, a Vancouver-based mortgage company had just been shut down by the regulatory authorities for taking $250,000,000 (that's sure a lot of zeros, isn't it?) from 10,000 separate investors. Each and every one of those 10,000 investors thought he was going to be warm and safe. It remains to be seen whether anyone will get a dime back.

Now here's the point: all of these 10,000 separate investors were small investors. Small investors are generally not knowledgeable enough or experienced enough to protect themselves, and (at least in this case) they put their faith where it doesn't belong. Of course, large investors are not immune to these kinds of mistakes. In fact, everyone would do well to remember this old Sicilian saying: "God protect me from my friends — I'll protect myself from my enemies."

So let's assume that you're not going to get embroiled in a syndicate-type investment, but instead are going to deal in individual pieces of property. This might mean buying a second home or a recreational property. Generally, a small investor buys only one or two units, while a larger investor might be looking for a tract of land to develop right away or to hold until the circumstances for development are more propitious.

WHY INVEST SMALL?

As a general rule, smaller investors have two main objectives: to make a capital gain and to have someone else pay the mortgage down. To make a capital gain, the key is to make the most money on the day you buy the property. It is a cold, harsh world out there, and you will not be forgiven if you make a buying mistake. That is why it is so important for the smaller investor to know his market extremely well. He has to look for the undervalued situation. He has to look for special circumstances, such as divorces, foreclosures, auctions, a motivated seller, and so forth. This is where the small investor actually has an advantage over the large investor. He's like that mongoose I mentioned earlier. He has speed and agility. He makes his own decisions, and thus can make them much more quickly. And he is more likely to be dealing with properties that are big enough to be interesting to him, but not big enough to be interesting to the large investor.

If the smaller investor knows his market well and has a clear understanding of current values, he can put that knowledge and understanding to very good use. But he has to be in the marketplace every day, and he has to step up to the plate with a constant stream of low offers. If you're not being turned down on nine out of ten of your offers, you're not an investor. You have to get used to being turned down to make sure you don't pay too much.

If the smaller investor is trying to have someone else reduce the mortgage, he may have to adjust his location objectives. Buying a $300,000 townhouse in a major metropolitan centre and renting it out for $1,200 doesn't make any sense if you're interested in cash flow — you have to hope for a capital gain in this situation. Buying a $110,000, fifteen-year-old bungalow with a basement suite in a smaller city, on the other hand, makes perfect sense. With even a minimum down payment and a fair mortgage rate, your payments will likely still be below $900 per month. But your income can be $1,500 — $1,100 from the main floor and $400 or so from the basement. I have seen small investors return 30 percent on deals like these, and these kinds of opportunities are still available.

While statistics show that the smaller investor always has more capital gain potential in single-family homes than in apartments, it is certainly possible to build a portfolio of apartments in smaller towns with low down payments, low mortgage payments, and a relatively high rental income. What the smaller investor needs to look for are apartments in the $35,000 to $65,000 range in a city with a good employment rate, low vacancies, and good growth potential (but study chapter 21 carefully, because there are some pitfalls).

As I'm writing this, you can quite easily go outside the large urban centres and buy a $50,000 unit with a rental income of $600 per month (this will pay the mortgage, taxes, and strata title fees). And here comes a very important point: Once the investor has this kind of property, he becomes like a buoy floating on the water. Inflation, deflation — it doesn't matter. Somebody else will pay down the mortgage for him. All he has to do is wait, and the clock and the calendar will work their magic.

The Empire of the Paper King

Let's talk about another class of small investor, the kind of person who buys a number of income-producing properties over time. I call this person the Paper King. He goes and buys a condominium in a small town for, say, $28,000 (yes, you can still do that!), fixes up the property with some cosmetic improvements, and ends up with a very presentable condominium that didn't cost very much money.

The Paper King then looks for a young couple in that area who have lots of character and no cash. He sells them the property for nothing down. (Yes, he gets credit reports. If they have just had their TV repossessed, he stops right there.) He may sell it for, say, $32,000, and he then carries back a second mortgage on the financing, which covers any money he's had to put into the property for the down payment, the cosmetic improvements, and his mark-up on the selling price.

And our Paper King just keeps doing this over and over again, thus building a significant portfolio of mortgage paper. I know of one of these people, and he likes to build his portfolio up to around $1.5 million and then go to a mortgage company and discount the paper. Although he may take a 10 or 15 percent discount for those mortgages, he gets his money up front, the lender gets a high yield, the young couple gets to own property, and everyone is happy with the transaction. The key, of course, lies in finding the right buyers. Be certain they will make the payments.

WHY INVEST LARGE?

The large investor has totally different objectives. Many are looking to buy a tract of land to develop. Indeed, buying land and subdividing it into lots has been the single biggest money-maker for the large investor and the large development corporation. Historically, these developers have been rewarded with profits far out of proportion to their original investment or their know-how.

More than any other type of investment, vacant-land investment, or land banking, has to involve smart purchases and good timing. Several very large corporations have been sunk by their land banks because their timing wasn't right. Remember that if you buy at the peak of the market, you have nowhere to go but down.

But when land banking works, it's beautiful. When a large investor has negotiating skills and the ability to thread his way through the red tape at city hall, he will reap the rewards. And these rewards are unusually high, sometimes 1000 percent or more! Of course, it goes without saying that those who do not have these skills will not reap these rewards. There doesn't seem to be a middle ground here. You either win or lose.

At a certain point, most larger investors start looking for portfolio diversification. Even those who invest largely in other fields want to have some real estate in their portfolios, and they look for income-producing properties such as apartment buildings, small shopping centres, plazas, small office buildings, etc. The most lucrative of these has quite often been the small shopping centre. Not only does this type of property provide cash flow in the 7 to 10 percent range, but it also appreciates in those areas that have population growth.

But as always, it's best to be cautious and well-informed. Values can depreciate not only in areas where people are leaving, but also in those where there is an over-ambitious anticipation of absorption. Take, for example, the situation of a developer who wants to put up a new office building. The construction process and wrangling with city hall could take three years or more. What happens if, in that time, market conditions shift? Suddenly, there's a glut of office space and rents have collapsed. But his building is half out of the ground and he has no choice except to complete it. This he does, even though he is going to be putting more unwanted space into a market that is already saturated.

Still, for the larger portfolio, these income-producing properties remain important. Mid-size regional shopping centres and small strip malls, for example, go for between $800,000 and $3 million, and they are very popular with mid-size offshore investors who want to be as close to downtown as possible. They will become increasingly important as the Real Estate Investment Trusts (REITs) absorb more and more quality income-producing property, without regard for return on investment.

REITs are a relatively new kind of large investor. They spring up in good times, so you hear a lot about them when things are humming. They started in a big way in the early 1980s, and then got clobbered in the savings-and-loan debacle. Right now, they are back with a vengeance. In Canada, some $6 billion went into hotel-type REITs, condo-type REITs, and commercial property REITs in 1997 alone. (For more on REITs, see chapter 17.)

HOW DO LARGE INVESTORS MAKE THEIR MONEY?

Larger investors often buy real estate wholesale and sell it retail. Therefore, in a vacant-land scenario, you buy by the acre and sell by the foot. In industrial areas, many investors will buy a site and, rather than building one large edifice for one large user, put up a group of mini-warehouses. Then they sell these off to individual owners.

It used to be that these kinds of warehouses would have only a 5 percent office component. But with downsizing and new company creation, things are changing. Warehouses now reserve 15 to 20 percent for office space, and small companies often find it possible to downsize into these smaller facilities and move the whole company there. Rather than having an office downtown and a warehouse in the suburbs, in other words, a small company can move into its own strata title warehouse (called an office complex).

So the lesson here is that a larger investor can make a much greater return by selling small pieces of a development to an end user. Some older office buildings downtown have actually been converted with this owner-user in mind. Also, larger investors benefit from having a greater understanding of industrial property in general. In most major areas of Canada, industrial vacancy rates were well below 4.5 percent in 1999, and values continued to rise. While some smaller astute investors can play, you generally need plenty of cash and staying power.

Are there other trends the large investor can exploit? Well, we're seeing more and more small, three-storey buildings with strata title stores on the ground floor and condos or apartments on top. Large investors are going to be doing more of this, because it is profitable and city councils like it. I believe there is limited depth-of-market appeal, but these properties have done well for the developer and larger investor.

I do not, however, recommend such a unit for the small investor as owner or user. Why? Well, the Strata Titles Act applies to the *whole* building. If you own a commercial space and share it with tenants, you will be liable for all the leaky roofs, tenant violations, and many other things you didn't bargain for. I expect to see a lot of disputes arising from these kinds of situations in the next five years.

So in my opinion, a larger investor should look at mini-warehouses, trailer parks, and mini-storage facilities. All of these have appreciation potential. All are cash cows. All have low overhead and none has tenant laws. A true millennium play.

In the end, the main similarity between small investors and large ones is that they both want more money. Unfortunately, the smaller investor has to run more risks to accomplish this.

In Essence

◇ A big investor can survive a small mistake, but a small investor can't survive a big mistake.

◇ If you're not being turned down on nine out of ten offers, you are not really an investor.

◇ Times and circumstances change. Both large and small investors have to be prepared to change with them.

◇ The closer the small investor is to the market, the better his chances for success. His agility is his advantage over the large investor.

5

Understanding Yourself

You can understand yourself only if you can be honest with yourself about yourself.

The title of this chapter should more accurately be "You Can't Understand Real Estate Investment Principles Until You Understand Yourself." I suppose you could, in theory, understand the principles from some objective standpoint if you didn't understand yourself, but that would be like being able to name all the tools in a tool box without being able to fix anything with them. You'd know enough to get started, but you wouldn't know enough to keep from hurting yourself. And that's what we're going to talk about in this chapter — doing yourself the most good (and its corollary: doing yourself the least harm).

So to be a successful investor, you have to take a good, hard look at yourself from a variety of perspectives — financial, intellectual, and temperamental. And of course, our emotions are an important part of the equation. Quite often, we hear the words "foreclosure," "auction," or "sealed-bid sales," for example, and we get so excited by the opportunity that we lose sight of the other elements of a successful deal (that is, work and risk). Almost every foreclosure I have participated in where the due diligence was done correctly (at least to my satisfaction) took almost a year before the deal was finalized. Indeed, judges usually bend over backwards in favour of the people who are being foreclosed on. You may have to work on ten foreclosures before you actually close on one. Do you have the temperament for that? Or do you have the temperament to evict the mother of three small children who has been deserted by her husband? (I hope not!) The point here is that these situations come up in this business, and it's important for you to know in advance what you can stomach and what you can't.

Knowing what kind of a person you are will tell you which situations to steer towards and which ones to steer away from. Some people, for example, take a visceral delight in the roller-coaster ride of certain kinds of deals. Good! They should find as many of them as they need. On the other hand, there are people who can't bring themselves to play liar's poker to see who is going to pay the lunch cheque. It is important that you know where you fit in. And the reason this is so important is that the more honest we are with ourselves, the more likely we are to match ourselves up with properties that will be what we expect. Almost all the unanticipated unhappiness in real estate investment comes from wishing instead of planning.

It has been my experience that, most of the time, people act without thinking. Worse yet, people are creatures of habit. People form their habits, and habits form their futures. If you don't deliberately form good habits, you unconsciously form bad ones. You are what you are because you have formed the habit of being your particular kind of person, and the only way you can change yourself is through changing your thinking and, with it, your habits.

Albert Einstein said, "Imagination is more important than knowledge." You have great imagination, so use it. Do some dreaming. If you don't, the penalty is a dreary life. I want to cause you to think in a new way about your life, your mind, your ability, your talent, and your imagination. And it all starts with trying to understand yourself, trying to become the person you want to be.

THE RICH GET RICHER . . .

Real estate investors who have money problems get involved with other real estate investors who have money problems. Owners of problem properties keep buying other problem properties. Landlords with tenant problems keep attracting problem tenants. Like attracts like. Most people go through life with preconceived ideas about people — and then they are bewildered when they attract the kind of people who occupy their minds. The challenge for you is to think, dream, plan, and travel your own road. The sooner you realize that today's results stem from yesterday's dreams, the more successful you'll be.

Of course, it's not always easy to figure out what we really want — in real estate or in life. People buy property in all kinds of places. And when they are asked how what they bought compared with what they started out looking for, they often answer that the two have little resemblance. For instance, many people buy units at ski resorts because they have a mental image of themselves getting personal use out of the place. They picture all the wonderful times they are going to have there, and of course imagine it all being paid for by the strangers who rent the property when they aren't there. The reality is that the high occupancy periods are the most desirable times, and it will cost the owners dearly to use those times for themselves. So they end up renting out the unit, and those wonderful mental pictures stay right where they started — in the imagination.

Would our would-be ski bunnies have paid the same amount for that property if they had looked at the deal with the objective eye of the investor rather than the romantic eye of the owner-user? Of course not. Being unaware of your own motivations can mean the difference between success and failure. Our ski bunnies would have been miles ahead if they'd bought a piece of rental property way below market value and used the profit to rent someone else's condo for two or three prime weeks a year.

DEFINE YOUR OBJECTIVES

By now, most everyone reading this will agree that investing in real estate requires work. And I hope you will also agree that the first work has to be done on yourselves. The first step is to define your investment objectives. What are you looking for? Is it cash flow? Do you want mortgage reduction to build up an equity base? Do you have staying power? Are you in for the long haul or are you a flipper? Do you enjoy the rough and tumble that often comes from interacting with people, or would you rather have passive situations where you'll be left alone? The answers to these questions will determine the kind of property you buy.

For example, let's say you have $20,000. In one scenario, you're a flipper who wants to turn over a property right away for a quick profit; in another, you are in for the long haul because you want to build up equity. If you are a flipper, you will look for a property that you can buy for well under the market and then resell at a quick profit. If you are a keeper, you should perhaps use your $20,000 for four $5,000 down payments on four condos that you can keep and rent out into the indefinite future. This second scenario works particularly well in inflationary times, while the first scenario works well if you find a motivated seller for whom time is a more critical factor than price.

But again, you have to look beyond dollars and cents and match the investment to your temperament. If you don't handle property problems well but have found a motivated seller with a problem property, you are not going to be a happy camper. If you don't handle people problems well and require eight hours of untroubled and uninterrupted sleep at night, those four condos in the low-rent district are not for you.

You need to ask yourself what kind of investor you are. How involved do you want to be? What are you good at? How much time do you have for this? What can you tolerate in terms of financial risk and people problems? The questions you ask yourself should not just be general, broad brushstrokes. You have to be specific and you have to be detailed.

You also have to know where you're starting from. If you're just starting out, you have a lot to learn. How much time and effort are you willing to devote to this? How much reading are you willing to do? Will you take courses? Will you go to seminars? What are you willing to do to fill in the blanks?

What about your investment objectives? Do you have a long- or short-term outlook? I know a man who has made a fortune in the California market and every purchase document of his is made out to "Nominee." That way, he can sell the property before he closes on it. Talk about short term! A long-term outlook might involve buying a piece of land with second-growth forest and literally growing yourself a million dollars. That would be long term in the extreme. But there's nothing wrong with extremes, so long as that is what suits your temperament and matches your investment objectives.

Your age is another factor. Your investment objectives at twenty-five will not be your investment objectives at sixty-five. If you're twenty-five, that property with the second-growth forest is the absolutely smartest thing you could buy. If you're sixty-five, you may hesitate before you buy green bananas. Again, what is important is that you have delineated your objectives and that you understand them.

THE FUTURE IS NOW

In real estate investment, there is no past and no present, only the future. So what you want to do is sit back, relax, and consider your greatest dream. Project yourself into the future. Picture yourself in five years as a successful investor. What does that mean to you? Do you have a portfolio of income-producing real estate? Are you the owner of a thousand-acre ranch? And the next step is to ask yourself what you did to achieve this. Did you trade your way up? Did you buy and hold and let the user of the property pay off the mortgage? Were you the hare or the tortoise?

As you may have guessed, all of this brings us full circle to understanding ourselves. If you don't go through the exercise of identifying exactly what kind of person you are, then you're going to be working with misconceptions. There is nothing worse than thinking that you're a person who has a great tolerance for risk, for example, then finding out that you can't sleep because worrying about your investment is keeping you awake.

If you don't fully understand yourself and your objectives, it is going to be more difficult for you to buy real estate successfully over the long term (note that I didn't say impossible). Let's say, for example, that you purchase some income-producing real estate so that someone else will pay off the mortgage and the equity build-up will add to your net worth. Then there is a downturn in the market. If your objectives are confused, you may lose heart and sell out. When the market turns again — as almost inevitably happens — you will be on the outside looking in.

If you had fully understood your objective — to have someone else pay down the mortgage — then it wouldn't really have mattered what the market was like. If the object of the exercise is to go from point A to point B in a canoe, then it doesn't matter how deep the water is as long as you're clear of the rocks on the bottom.

My point here, obviously, is that you must ask yourself some tough questions and answer them fully and truthfully before you buy. I have seen hundreds of people whose lives changed dramatically once they grasped the concept of understanding themselves and their investment objectives. In fact, I think this is so crucial that I will send you a tape of a speech I made called "17 Success Secrets of Top-Producing People" for the price of shipping alone. (Call 1-800-691-1183 for shipping instructions.)

In the meantime, take a look at your personal weaknesses and strengths. Ask some of your friends and relatives what they perceive your strengths and weaknesses to be (though be prepared, because you may not like what you hear). Ask the same question of current and former business associates. You'll probably get the most truthful answer from the former associate.

Now admittedly, this quest for self-awareness is not easy. And yes, you can live your whole life without it. After all, if you don't know what you're missing, you won't notice any difference. But the people who do notice the difference are the ones who know the value of self-knowledge and do the work that is necessary to attain it. They're also the ones who leave the others behind in the dust.

Do the work. Create the difference. You'll see how that difference will work for you.

In Essence

◇ You can't understand real estate investment principles until you understand yourself.
◇ Like attracts like.
◇ Two percent of the people think, 3 percent of the people think they think, and 95 percent would rather die than think.
◇ You can't get useful answers if you don't ask the right questions.
◇ Knowing what you don't know is more important than knowing what you know.

6

The Three Ways
to Lose Money
in Real Estate

*Don't go around saying the world owes you a living. The
world owes you nothing; it was here first.*

— MARK TWAIN

There are myriad ways to make money in real estate, and it can take
a lifetime to learn all of them. On the other hand, there are only
three ways to lose money in real estate — greed, ignorance, and bad
luck — and you can put all of them into effect the first day.

Now, I strongly believe that this is where this book can probably be
of the most use. There are shelves full of books on how to make money
in real estate, but very few that point out how you can lose it. And of
course, any loss involves more than just money. Setbacks of this nature
also cost you time (the time it took you to make the money in the first

place *and* the time it will take you to earn it back) and emotional strength. When people talk about real estate losses, everyone concentrates on the money factor and practically no mention is made of the time factor or the emotion factor. Well, we're going to cover the whole spectrum.

TWO CATEGORIES OF LOSS

Losses fall into two main categories: category number one covers losses that occur when you should (and could) have known better, and category number two covers those that occur when you were just at the wrong place at the wrong time.

Let's look at an example. You're an Edmonton resident who just bought your dream home in January. In February, your boss comes into your office with a big smile on her face and informs you that you're taking over the Halifax office in March. You put your newly acquired house on the market, and to nobody's surprise it doesn't bring what you paid for it.

So what category of loss is this? Well, maybe both. You knew when you bought the property that you would have to own it for at least five years to outlive the vagaries of the marketplace and be in profit. But all of a sudden, you became what we call situationally or circumstantially disadvantaged, and you're going to lose money as a result. That makes this a category-two loss. There was nothing you could have done to predict it, right? Or was there? If you had looked ahead and foreseen this possibility, you would have addressed it in your employment contract (then the loss would be your company's). That makes this a category-one loss.

We get caught up in all kinds of situations, and sometimes they are beyond our control. But most of the time, we *should* have known better because we *could* have known better. Of course, all of us are blessed with 20/20 hindsight. But what we want to talk about here are some of those situations that could have been avoided had we used some of that very uncommon common sense. (In a later chapter, we'll talk about what to do when the unavoidable problem actually happens.)

We so often see people take their hard-earned money and, without much thought, give it to someone who promises them a better world. This falls under the auspices of the number-two way to lose money in real estate: ignorance. Why would you, having never really gambled in your life, take your money and give it to a total stranger simply on the promise of performance in the future? I know I have said time and time again that track record is not necessarily a guarantee of future performance, but I cringe when I see new companies making the most outlandish promises and people stampeding to hand over their money. These are brand-new companies with no track record at all!

Now, I'm not talking rocket science here — I'm talking about very basic common sense. Let's say someone comes along and says he is going to earn you a certain percentage return (the actual figure doesn't matter, so long as it's high enough to be attractive). Why do you believe him? Well, what he is appealing to is that little piece of your heart that wants to engage in larceny (that's right, theft!). Remember: you can't cheat an honest man. That's a fact.

But why is that a fact? Well, an honest man knows that there is no such thing as a free lunch. An honest man knows that anything to do with money is a zero-sum game (which means that whatever one person wins, some other person has to lose). So in a world of 6 or 7 percent returns, a promised return of 25 percent should have all the appeal of a fish that has been lying on the dock for three days. But what happens to the rest of us? *Our greed overrides our common sense.* And so, without asking even the simplest questions, we throw our money into the fire. Let's look at a typical example.

A company places a big ad announcing that, on a certain date, it will be having a seminar to reveal how you can have a real estate investment that will pay you 24 percent returns with complete safety. All you've got to do to find this particular financial Holy Grail is go to this seminar.

So you go to the seminar. Someone stands up on a platform and tells you how he is going to buy something at one price and, sometime later, sell it at another price. If you will give him the money to make this possible, he will pay you 24 percent for the use of it. You are interested, so you fill in a card with your name, address, and phone number. A few days later, you get a call from someone in the organization and arrange to go down to the office to discuss things in a little more detail.

It's a very swanky office indeed — deep carpets, rosewood panelling, expensive furniture, computers humming, phones ringing, employees hustling hither and yon. It looks good. You're taken in to get more of the pitch. You're not really getting a lot of substance, but that's okay because all you really care about is that number they keep throwing at you: 24 percent. Of course, their offering memorandum (OM) also states that commissions total 10 to 17 percent. Yet still you hand over your life's savings. Then you go home and wait for the cheques to start coming in.

And they do come in for a while, but one day they stop. You contact the company and get an explanation. Nothing changes. You contact the company again and get some excuses. Then one morning, you pick up your newspaper and read that the company you gave your money to has been handed a cease-and-desist order by one of the many government agencies that are supposed to regulate the industry, and the yogurt is starting to hit the fan.

You make more phone calls, and get more explanations and more excuses. Out of fear, you elect to believe that everything is going to be all right. But as weeks and then months pass, with more newspaper articles on how the company is defunct, you start to realize that you might as well have done the whole deal on a handshake. The reality of your situation starts to sink in, and you lapse into a state of shock.

There we have just one scenario from start to finish. The question is, How could this tragedy have been avoided? Let's go back to the newspaper ad that started the entire process. Twenty-four percent? First common-sense question: How can a company pay 24 percent when first mortgage money is 7 percent and second mortgage money is 10 percent? If the basic tenet of business — that risk has to equal return — is valid, then doesn't it stand to reason that the reverse of the equation — that return has to equal risk — is just as valid? If they are offering me a 24 percent return, are they not also asking me to undertake a 24 percent risk?

But let's say I ignore this particular red flag and still attend the seminar. The newspaper ad that brought me in cost thousands of dollars. They hired that big ballroom in the hotel, gave me brochures, and paid a speaker to stand up at the microphone and do his song and dance. This also cost thousands of dollars. But who's paying for all this? I am. All of this money has to come out of my investment dollar before it goes to work.

Still, let's say I also ignore this other red flag and go to the office. All that rent. All those expenses. The salaries for all those people. The commissions to all those salesmen. A prudent person would know that he shouldn't be putting his money into something like this.

But even if I ignore all this, there are other questions I should be asking myself. What is this property that I'm investing in worth today, and who says that's what it's worth? Is there a valid independent appraisal? Was the property acquired at arm's length, or are there layers of interlocking companies with undisclosed fees and commissions and mark-ups? Again, a prudent person would deduce that at least twenty-five to forty cents out of every dollar was coming off the top before the money was even starting to be put to work. That means that the sixty cents that was left would have to earn more than 100 percent for you to get back that $1.24 at the end of one year.

And what about track record? How long have these people been in business? You will find, almost without exception, that these companies are new and that they have not had even one successful business cycle. (By that, I mean that they don't have a list of investors who went into a project and came out the other side with profit in hand.) They will point to people who are currently enjoying the promised results, but close examination will reveal that these investors are being paid with the money of the new investors. This is what is known as a Ponzi scheme, and it generally motors along just fine right up until it collapses.

DON'T LET IGNORANCE BE YOUR GUIDE

But what happens, you may be saying, if I don't know what questions to ask? You do the same thing you do in every other aspect of your life. You don't make your own clothes, do you? Do you cut your own hair or repair your own car? No, you go to a professional. I can't understand why people will spend all kinds of money on every kind of professional advice, but they will not buy any of the readily available expertise in the financial fields.

Any knowledgeable financial adviser who can hear thunder and see lightning would have been able to assess the Ponzi scheme I just described and would have told you to take a pass. But if you really object to paying someone $200 for an hour of her time, you can take a course at the local real estate board, attend a teaching seminar (*not* a selling seminar), or even get a book out of the library. Don't let ignorance be your guide. And don't assume, as many people do, that the government is protecting you from your own foolishness. Nothing could be further from the truth. The government is there to prosecute wrongdoers when they bob to the surface, but you're going to have to protect yourself.

Ignorance isn't an excuse, a defence, or the basis on which some government agency is going to give you back your money. As I've already said, if it is possible for you to know, then it is your responsibility to know. And most of the time, basic precautions are all that is necessary.

I hope that the very fact that you are reading this book means that you want to educate yourself. So let's consider a few more basic steps you can take to protect your estate purchases. The most important of all these is the appraisal of the property. The appraisal is based on comparisons of your property with recently sold properties that were similar in nature. You should compare the property you are considering with at least three that have just sold, three that are still on the market, and three whose listings expired before they sold.

What's crucial here is that the properties with which you're comparing yours are recent and similar. The comparables used should not be older than sixty days (the only exceptions are rare out-of-town or special-property situations where older comparables must do), and they should be similarly located and the same style, size, etc. (Any knowledgeable real estate practitioner should be able to get you this information with a few clicks of her mouse.)

Of course, all the appraisal tells you is if the price is right. If you want to know more (and you should!), you have to go deeper. Where does the property stand compared with its immediate neighbours? Is it the better house on the poorer street or the other way around? If you're looking at a unit in a strata building, you must get a copy of the previous twelve months of strata council minutes. Strata councils usually wash their dirty linen at the council meetings. If they don't want to give the minutes to you, walk away. You need to know what roof repairs are pending, what's breaking down, who's breaking in, and what monies are in the contingency fund to cover it all.

You've got to ask those questions and make those comparisons and do the necessary research. If you want the returns and the safety that a professional investor gets, you're going to have to do what a professional investor does. You've got to dig until you know as much as it is possible to know. But don't expect all of this to come easy at the start. At first this is unfamiliar territory, but after three months of looking at specific properties in a specific area, you'll be able to make your own value judgements.

BECOME YOUR OWN EXPERT

When I look at the various mortgage companies and funds that have gone down in the past   and at those that are in the process of going down even as I write this — I am filled with sadness for all those thousands of people who have lost money. It is all so unnecessary and all so easily avoided. You must learn which questions to ask and recognize when the answers are valid. When you do this, you become your own expert. Then you're in an even better position to use the advice of the real experts to help you maximize your results.

We also all have some common sense, and if we put that common sense to work, it alone can keep us out of a lot of trouble. I'm a great believer in gut feelings (once you're grounded in a certain amount of basic knowledge, of course). And I also believe that it doesn't matter how many good deals you turn down — what matters is staying out of the bad ones.

Of course, one of the big dangers with buying property is that any mistake you make doesn't have to be very large to be fatal. For example, I personally know about seven different investors who, as I write this, are caught in traps of their own making. They bought too many properties for their circumstances. Although the monthly negative cash flow for each is only between $1,000 and $3,000, that is enough to break them. What got each one into trouble was a combination of ignorance and greed.

But what of bad luck, the third way to lose money in real estate? Bad luck is what happens when you did your due diligence, hired good people, had a good project in a good area, and still lost money. In most instances, this is more a question of timing than anything else.

In the early 1980s, for example, you could have put your money in with some very fine, honest people who had great successes in the past, and you still would probably have been wiped out when the markets collapsed. It happened to everyone — from the largest real estate companies in North America to the smallest individual investors. The only people who survived were those with paid-off property or those who were between deals and were sitting on cash. (Guess what they did with that cash once the market bottomed out?)

Bad luck comes in all kinds of packages. You could find, for instance, that the good investment property you bought has suddenly been rezoned or put under some non-conforming covenant that reduces its value. Generally speaking, however, you can avoid bad luck simply by owning the property outright in your own name. If you own the property free and clear, you usually just have to wait out any storms. But if you're relying on the upward motion of inflation and you're highly leveraged, your financial survival will depend on your staying power.

Bad luck really kills you if you're in bed with someone whose situation is worse than yours, such as a developer who gets caught by the ticking time bomb of interest payments on his mortgages. Or let's say you put money in with a good developer who has the best of intentions and a good business plan, only to find that the units don't sell as projected. All the profits are eroded because the market conditions stretch out the sales period. The most frustrating thing about being caught in this kind of situation is that you can't do anything to ameliorate it. You'll just be swept along by the forces at play until those forces change or you have nothing left to lose.

Ignorance, greed, bad luck. Correcting the first and controlling the second will help you avoid the third.

In Essence

◇ You can't cheat an honest man.
◇ Risk should at least equal return. It can be more, but it can't be less.
> There's expertise available to help you make informed decisions. Use it.
> People think the government is protecting them from their own ignorance. Nothing could be further from the truth.

7

The Personal Real Estate Investment Action Plan

The thought is father to the deed.

Following an investment plan that is not personal to you is like wearing somebody else's tailor-made suit. No matter what you do, it isn't going to fit as well as it should. If you want optimum results, it all starts with the personal plan.

In real estate, or any other area of investment, the average person looks for formula solutions. We want to take the shortcut of somebody else's solution rather than devising a route for ourselves. As a result, most of us go through our lives looking for somebody else to give us the answer, some guru to follow. We search around for somebody to trust, and when we think we've located such a person, we cheerfully hand over all our money and hope he will do a good job.

Such a course of action is fraught with danger, but avoiding that danger is relatively simple. All you have to do is sit down with a piece of paper and list some serious questions. Are you buying for cash flow? Do you need to make an investment that brings you a cash-on-cash return (i.e., that gives you spendable cash as compensation for the money you have invested), or are you more interested in building equity? It's like peeling away one layer of an onion to reveal the layer beneath.

For example, if you have $1 million to invest and you need cash on cash, you're going to have to buy a property with the terms arranged so that it will have a small enough mortgage to yield the cash flow that you require. If you have no need for cash flow, you can buy a larger property with a larger mortgage and let the tenant of that property pay off that mortgage. In that scenario, your return will be in capital appreciation.

The next question to ask is where you are in the current cycle of investment. Where do you put yourself in the scheme of what is happening in the world? Can you see more inflation on the horizon or less? What are your personal objectives? Are you acquiring a property for a specific purpose? If so, will the property serve that purpose? Remember that you put yourself in whatever position you want to be in, and that you do it through what you think is going to happen. If you can spot a trend before it happens or when it just starts, it can result in a very handsome payoff. In each and every case, you have to decide what you think is going to happen, then you have to act on it.

WHY IS A WRITTEN PLAN IMPORTANT?

Once you have decided what you think will happen, you have to construct a plan of action. This will be your personal real estate investment action plan! Remember that today's realities stem from the dreams of the past (or lack thereof). The seeds you planted in the past are what you're harvesting today, and it all started with an idea. It is crucial to realize that your dreams determine your expectation of the future. It is almost like a mathematical formula — if the dream is connected to a plan and the plan is connected to an action, then the action will be connected to reality.

When you have the dream in focus, decide on a set of steps that will move you towards your goal. If income is the goal, you'll want one kind of real estate. If the goal is growth, then you will want another. But in any case, you'll want to do it step by step. And each step that you take should move you closer to your goal. I call this the Doctrine of the Next Specific. In any course of action, there is one specific act that is the most important and therefore it is that act that should be done next. If you apply this to your action plan, you will, by definition, always be working on exactly what you should be working on.

One of the chief advantages of the written action plan is that it's always easy to remind yourself where you're going. And if your way gets blocked, you are better able to adjust your course and try again. But remember that if you make a change in the plan, you must write it down (so the change becomes part of the new plan). We don't plan to fail, of course, unless we fail to plan.

Once you have decided on your main goal, you must ask yourself what kind of game you really want to play. Are you clear on what your risk tolerance is? Almost nothing is worse than sitting down to what you think is one kind of game and then finding that you are in a totally different one. What happens if you purchase a property and find out after the fact that you have to feed it $500 a month because that's your mortgage shortfall, or you can't rent it, or the tenant leaves you with a lot of repairs? Can your personal financial position support that?

Try to get these and any other variables you can think of jotted down on paper. Asking yourself these questions will tell you what kind of properties you can buy. You need to be able to match up your investment objectives and your temperament in the properties you buy. If you don't need cash flow, for example, and want lots of safety as you build equity, then you may want to make a larger down payment on a smaller property and let all the rental income go towards paying down the mortgage. But if you think that inflation is about to come back, then you may want to buy the biggest property you can find for the lowest down payment. Either way, the objective should be to construct a set of goals so that you have a plan or a template to follow. And again, you've got to write these goals down. Goals and plans that are not written down are nothing but musings.

According to Tony Robbins, a 1950s Stanford University study followed students for a twenty-year period and examined their goal-setting habits. Only 7 percent of these students consistently wrote down their goals. Like magic, those who wrote them down ended up as the heads of companies and the leaders in their professions. There were also some outstanding successes among the remaining 93 percent, but the majority were just average. Obviously, the lesson here is that you have a better chance of excelling if you put your goals in writing.

Of course, just writing down the goals is not enough. The key to the whole process is taking action. We spend an infinitesimally small amount of our time acting and all the rest of it reacting. We react to situations, to circumstances, and to other people's actions because we feel we have to. But the real change, the real forward progress, comes from taking action, and the best kind of action to take is the action that is planned.

I know I have said this before, but I really must stress that there is one factor that is common to all successful action plans: they are all written down! *If you don't write it down, it isn't an action plan.* Create a goal from your dreams, devise an action plan, write it down, and commit yourself to it. Then measure your results, and change and adapt as necessary.

Almost without exception, the really successful people I know are list-makers. They need a result-measuring stick. The process of writing something down defines and crystallizes the goal. Once you have your action plan written down, you will be able to ascertain when you're proceeding in the right direction and when you've strayed off-track. You can consider each proposed action in the light of the plan as a whole. Is this next step going to be a forward step or is it going to be a detour? Does this property I'm considering fit my overall investment objectives? Once you've done this, it's easy to evaluate the situations that come your way. Then you either act on them or discard them.

GOALS MUST BE SPECIFIC AND MEASURABLE

To really get the most of your action plan, you must set specific, easily evaluated goals. "I want to make a lot of money" is *not* a goal. "I will work hard" is *not* an action plan.

"I will buy one property for less than $60,000 with no money down. The income must carry all expenses. I will buy it between October 1 and December 31." Now *that* is a clearly defined goal. And so is this: "I will have an income of $5,500 per month by January 1, 2008, and I will achieve it by buying eleven properties by January 1, 2004. All properties must clear $500 per month by January 1, 2008." Goals like these force you to write down how you actually intend to get there.

The planner is ahead of the game. He knows that following the plan leads to success. So why doesn't everyone do it? I can show you the greatest business plan in the world, one that will take you right to where you want to be, guaranteed, but I can't make you follow it. You have to have the discipline to start for yourself.

You also have to have a lot of energy, and energy flows to where your concentration goes. A good action plan helps you focus on your objectives. Ask yourself what you are concentrating on. What are you giving your energy to? What are you surrendering to? What is your alignment? What do you talk about? What do you complain about? This all takes needed energy!

Once you've learned to redirect your energy and focus your concentration, the next step is to get out into the field. Nothing will take the place of personal, hands-on examination of whatever property interests you. Nothing will give you a more accurate frame of reference than doing this yourself. If you don't believe this, stop reading right here. Not only can't I help you, but I can also practically guarantee that you will make some horrendously expensive mistakes.

Well, you're still reading, so I guess we're agreed. We're going to get out into the field. If you plan to deal directly with owners, be sure you learn the ins and outs. If you plan to deal with a realtor, connect up with a quality agent. In fact, get on the lists of a number of quality realtors who specialize in a lot of different areas. Tell them what your parameters are, being specific and definite. Once a realtor knows what you want, she won't waste your time, or hers, with anything that is outside your area of interest.

For example, you could tell the realtor that all you want are properties from divorces, executive transfers, foreclosures, auctions, or any circumstance that will motivate a seller to deal. Or you could say all you want are "low down payment" situations. Once you have a relationship with the realtor, respond quickly to whatever she brings you. If she perceives you as someone who will give a quick no if the answer is no and a quick yes followed by decisive action if the answer is yes, you will be on her A-list. You want to be on that list so that you can see what she has as soon as she gets it.

Once the agent starts showing you properties, the next steps are to decide where to buy in relation to the prices possible and the tenants available, and to do the due diligence. Due diligence of a real personal action plan includes details like this:

- I will research which will be the best city to buy in between November 1, 2000, and February 1, 2001.
- I will get the official CMHC vacancy statistics for the target cities by October 31, 2000 (these are published every October for every city in Canada for every class of property).
- I will get, by October 31, 2000, the StatsCan and provincial stats to show the expected population growth is in the city I selected.
- I will get school-board statistics to see if grade 1 registration is increasing or decreasing in the area.

These four simple steps will, by themselves, tell you what kind of tenant base you can expect to have. That way, you'll have an idea of what to expect from the various kinds of rental properties in the area.

There are all kinds of help out there just waiting for you. Stationery stores have forms that are designed for evaluating rental property. If you can't find what you want, go to the library. Or ask your realtor for a copy of the evaluation form she uses and use that as a basis.

There are very few things in this business that I am as sure of as this: If you sit down, analyze your objectives, and then write them down, you will become a successful investor. Your action plan is like a compass that will take you to where you want to go. But please don't craft a great written plan and then shove it in a drawer and forget it. It has to be something that you are continually working on, adding to, and adapting. The person who does this will progress farther and faster than people who are richer and smarter and better connected. It is the single most important thing you can do.

In Essence

◇ Your action plan helps you determine what kind of a game you want to play.
◇ One of the single most important factors to determine is your risk tolerance.
◇ You've got to know where you're starting from before you can map a route to where you want to go.
◇ The next step you take — whatever it is — is the most important.
◇ Your action plan doesn't have to be perfect from the start. You're going to be fine-tuning it as you go along.

8

The Importance of
Doing It Yourself

If you want a job done right, do it yourself. If things turn out badly, at least you'll know who to blame.

Most of the successful, productive people I have encountered in my business activities have been very structured. Often, they have very big — even grandiose — dreams. In my view, there is nothing wrong with that. I've yet to meet a top-producing investor who dreams of owning a tiny house in a bad neighbourhood. They all want to have that larger car, that bigger house. Yet usually what drives these people isn't the money per se — it's the game itself. The money is just the way they keep score.

You should be careful about dreaming too small a dream, because that's all you may get. You may leave a lot of chips on the table just because you aimed too low. And of course, once you're in the game and playing it successfully, it takes the same amount of work to go after the larger goal. I would even submit that, generally speaking, the larger the investment, the less emotion is involved. Thus the investor who is buying a hotel or a shopping centre almost has less at stake emotionally than the individual buying a vacation property for personal use. This is because the large investor has approached the game rationally and logically. He understands yields and cash flow and cap rates, and knows the specific goals he wishes to achieve down to the last percentile.

Let's take, for example, an investor named John who has a million dollars in cash but isn't interested in taking any inordinate risks. To minimize risk, John might put 3 percent in the bank, 5 percent in bonds, and maybe 6 percent in a shopping centre. That shopping centre represents the maximum amount of "risk" that John is willing to allow into his portfolio. For some people, this would be too high; for others, it would be too low. But for John, it is just right. John has to decide these ratios for himself.

How does he do this? Well, he measures the problems and the costs of dealing with tenants; weighs these against the calculated income, the capital appreciation, and whatever tax benefits there may be for him; and then comes to a decision about whether to proceed. He can seek all kinds of advice from all kinds of experts and consultants, but the actual decision has to be made by him, the man who is writing the cheque.

Now, the degree to which he can control his emotions is the degree to which he improves his chances of making the right decision. When it comes to a shopping centre, everybody agrees with this approach. But for some mysterious reason, when we come to residential investment property all sorts of emotional factors start to seep in. Yet if we take the same approach to the small investment as we do to the large one, we are less likely to make a mistake.

THINK LIKE A BIG INVESTOR EVEN IF YOU'RE BUYING SMALL

The careful investors on the larger end are always asking questions. What are the risks? Do I really want to do this? Is there something better I could be doing with this money? They want to have written copies of leases for their tenants, and they study these leases with their lawyers. They want to understand the zoning requirements. What are the parking restrictions? What can city officials do in the future? What are they precluded from doing?

You should do the same thing even if you're buying a single-family home as an investment. *Ask questions.* If the answers you get don't match the facts, or even if you just don't like the answers, find out why. And do all of this before you buy — because it's too late after. In real estate investment, the money you don't lose is twice as important as the money you win.

It is equally important that you not rely on anyone else for this information unless you trust that person implicitly. If you go into a brand new neighbourhood, find a brand-new salesman, and then accept everything he tells you at face value, you may as well just pile all your money on the table and set fire to it.

Let's say, for example, that you find a very acceptable subdivision in a small town some distance from where you live. You purchase a property that is the right price and looks good. What you don't know is that your unit is built on clay and your basement is likely to flood. Every owner with a unit like yours is going to have problems. Not surprisingly, all the prospective owners who did their due diligence invested some-place else. This proves the importance of doing what needs to be done — and doing it yourself.

It is crucial to inspect the property yourself. Don't convince your-self that you don't have the time to do this. Even the big guys lose money on properties that were not personally inspected. Nothing is more important than this. In fact, if you are such a captain of industry that you can't find time to inspect a property, don't buy it. Wait until you can. This is particularly true in the case of a long-distance purchase. Too often you'll find that a property that looks very good on paper backs on to a garbage dump in reality.

I have a developer friend who bought a property from pictures that were shown to him. The pictures showed a beautiful screen of tall deciduous trees. But when the trees lost their leaves, they revealed a city works yard with all the heavy equipment rusting away — not a pretty sight. Had my friend inspected the site personally, he would have been aware of this. Our number-one principle is that you make the most money on the day you buy, and the amount is dictated by how effectively you do your due diligence.

IT'S NOT LOCATION, LOCATION, LOCATION . . . IT'S VALUE, VALUE, VALUE

If I were to buy a single home for an investment, I'd look to buy a cheaper home on a more expensive street, but never the other way around. There is a levelling dynamic that sees more expensive homes get pulled down to the median and less expensive ones get pulled up. We've all seen cases where someone puts up an elaborate mansion in a fairly good neighbourhood and then can't resell it because people who buy mansions want to live in a neighbourhood with other mansions. Still, that mansion will have a positive effect on the less expensive houses on the block.

Absolutely everything — highways, road noises, gas stations, etc. — has an effect on value. Most planning departments have a wealth of information, so a quick trip to city hall is always advisable. And the key here again is to question, question, question. Are there major zoning changes contemplated? Is there going to be a change in any of the streets? Get your hands on whatever documentation you can. Don't take anybody's word for these things.

What you don't want is to have a four-lane highway coming down the road towards you and winding up in your front yard. Still, changes are sometimes beneficial. A new shopping centre, golf course, or some other kind of development might turn out to be a big benefit. If you know about these things, you can cut your cloth accordingly.

Will Rogers used to say that the secret was to find out where people were going and then get there before them and buy the real estate. Conversely, if you see people leaving an area — for any reason — that's not a place where you want to be buying. Real estate values are determined by demand. If people are leaving, you are not going to realize any capital appreciation.

Tell yourself that you will invest only in deals where you can lose small but win big. Never invest if you can win small but lose big. You should also try to start small and build from there. Upgrade with each successive purchase.

Remember also that you need to structure your deal properly at the start. Whenever you enter into negotiations to buy a property, you want to make sure that you give yourself enough time in your purchase agreement to investigate the title completely. I know of one case where a utility company had an easement over a piece of property and the owner had to remove a three-car garage. In another case, someone bought a large tract of property for a subdivision development and found that one of the homeowners on an adjoining development had built a tennis court on his property. It was a windfall for the new owner of the tract, but it was very distressing for the owner of the tennis court.

I've repeated it so often it is becoming like a mantra, but I'll say again that you make the most money on the day you buy your property. The time you take doing your own due diligence can only add to the value. Indeed, the only time you might be able to get away without doing due diligence is during a period of high inflation, when you are flipping properties and getting in and out in a very short span of time.

In one of my lectures, I commented on the importance of doing the due diligence personally, and one of the men in the audience asked, "You mean, I should inspect a property even if it is in the United States?" It turned out that this man, who was considering investing between $60,000 and $100,000 or more, was balking at spending $500 on a plane ticket to do his own inspection!

Go and see the property. Quite often, that picture of the graceful palm tree in front of that Phoenix property is two decades old and the tree has since suffered twenty years of neglect. Go there, look at it, kick the tires. Once you get there, you might find an entirely different property that will be a much better investment. Also, you have to bear in mind that if you're investing outside your area, the people who are presenting you with properties are going to show you only what they have in their wagon. They're not going to go out of their way for a stranger unless they're assured a piece of the deal.

In my view, it is always better to buy locally, because you can do your due diligence easily and deal with a local realtor. If you live in Toronto and want to buy in Phoenix, however, get in touch with a Phoenix realtor, particularly if someone in Canada is trying to sell you a packaged deal. The local realtor has the proper perspective. (But when it comes time to sell, by all means sell that Phoenix property in Toronto — you'll get a better price than you would in Phoenix. So buy local but sell long distance.)

A FOOL AND HIS MONEY ARE SOON PARTED

I believe it's also important to do things yourself when it comes time to make an offer. A lot of agents will discourage this, because they want to be the intermediaries, but there's nothing wrong as long as you are controlling the process. In fact, the more experienced you get at this, the closer you're going to want to be to it. Sometimes a raised eyebrow on the other side of the table can translate into tens of thousands of dollars if you're there to see it.

And here I want to repeat a claim that I have made before: If you don't make ten offers for every one property you buy — which means being turned down nine times — you are not what I call an investor.

You're just someone who owns property for which he paid too much. Now, I've had investors tell me that their realtor doesn't like to write low offers. If this is the case, I have only one piece of advice: fire your realtor. Remember that the average commission on a $200,000 condo is $10,000. For $10,000, a realtor — *any* realtor — should be willing to write offers all day and all night.

When you're making an offer, be sure to control your emotional involvement. Objectivity is easier when you are not the owner-user, of course, but you should strive for it whatever the circumstances. As soon as you become emotionally involved, two things happen. First, you start to lose right away, because whoever cares least has the advantage. And second, you are no longer open and receptive to other — and possibly better — opportunities.

Another reason that objectivity is so important is that it helps you maintain a healthy scepticism. If a deal looks extra-super-special, that is the time to take out the scepticism magnifying glass. Why am I so lucky? Why is someone offering an 18 percent return or selling below market price? You've got to ask and ask and ask. And then — and this is one of the most important concepts in this book — after you've asked the questions, shut up and listen to the answers! You'll be amazed what you can learn from an owner if you ask the right questions. Very often, in fact, he will tell you much more than he ought to. This is another reason to do this part yourself instead of leaving it to your agent.

And don't be afraid to ask very basic questions, such as, "What are you going to do with this money I'm going to pay you?" If the owner answers that he's going to put it in a mutual fund that invests in mortgages, maybe he'll be willing to carry the mortgage on his own property. That could mean that certain points and brokerage fees could be eliminated, and the two of you could divide that money. Or if he's not going to spend the money on something right away, maybe he'll take a lower down payment or a deferred down payment.

Will he include the stove and fridge? What about the freezer in the garage? And don't stop there — find out what's going to happen to all the furniture in the house. I know a man who runs a thrift shop for the Wildlife Society. He told me that people will often call him to get the contents of a house when they are moving out of the country or are downsizing to a condo or an apartment. He has a whole section of his thrift store full of gardening tools and lawnmowers that he obtained for nothing. If the purchaser of the property had only asked, he probably could have had all of those chattels included in the deal.

Here's another gem. People always want to know why someone is selling a property, but almost nobody asks why a seller bought the property in the first place. His reasons for purchasing will help you define the market you'll be aiming at when the time comes for you to sell.

Finally, expect everything that you do yourself to be hard work. There are no free lunches. Every time you make an offer and are turned down, you're going to learn something. And you will include that information in your personal action plan. If you don't find sellers who fit into your formula, just keep looking. Eventually, you'll either find the person you're looking for, or you'll learn to adapt your formula to fit the reality. Someone once said that the secret to happiness was to strive for excellence but be prepared to lower your standards until they coincided with what was available. If you don't want to lower those standards, just stay on the sidelines and watch the game from there until the time is right.

In the final analysis, any deal you make has to make sense to you. And so, as selfish as this may seem, you are the only one who matters. That is why you have to do the important stuff yourself.

In Essence

> Important decisions should be made by the person who is writing the cheque.
> If you have to lose, lose small. When you win, win big.
> The more careful an investor you are, the more questions you're going to ask.

◇ Structure your deal properly before you start.
◇ The money you don't lose is twice as important as the money you win.
◇ Don't take shortcuts. That's real money you're using — or maybe losing.

9

The Art
of the Deal

The asking price for a piece of property is the absolute wildest dream of the seller.

Structuring a real estate deal is much more an art than a craft — and it certainly isn't a science. You can make (i.e., save) or lose a lot of money in how you structure your deal. In fact, the proper structure often will mean the difference between being able to buy a property or not being able to buy it.

Early in my career, I ran across a real estate book titled *There Are a Hundred Ways to Buy Real Estate — Cash Is One of Them*. It's important to bear that in mind. Any dummy can buy property for the full asking price if he's willing to write a cheque for that amount. As a matter of fact, if you're willing to pay full price, then you need learn nothing more about real estate! But if you want to do it some other way, you're going to be involved in the art of the deal. Remember that in life, you do not get what you deserve — you get what you negotiate.

You don't want to do things backwards. You don't want to select the ideal property, in other words, and then see how you can tailor the deal. What you want to do is to construct an idea of the deal you want to make and then go shopping for properties that will fit within the parameters you've set. The most common formula is to select a property, find out how much of a mortgage you can arrange, put in the difference in cash, and there's your deal. That's how most properties are bought and sold, so let's start by examining some of the components of this equation.

UNDERSTANDING THE EQUATION

To begin this exercise, let's work from the perspective of the buyer. Later on, we'll take the stance of the seller.

So there are six main components to the equation, as follows:

- the price;
- the terms;
- the mortgage amount;
- the mortgage rate;
- the mortgage term;
- the source of the money.

In addition, you must bear in mind three questions: Who will do what? Who will own what? and What about the commission? All of these factors are going to be dealt with in the negotiations. Although the vendor and the vendor's agent may think that the only deal possible is for full price and all cash, the negotiations are going to create certain modifications of this position. Most of these modifications are going to be determined by the motivation of the seller, which is one of the most important variables in the equation.

The Price

If you think about it, the asking price is the seller's way of telling you the absolute most money that he will accept for his property. This is the way you should approach asking prices — as a starting point. The same goes for your first offer, which is really just your own wildest fantasy. If any vendor ever said yes to any purchaser's opening offer, it would create a panic! The purchaser would immediately suspect that he had missed something and would want to re-examine the deal.

The usual scenario is that purchaser and vendor meet somewhere in the middle. One of my mentors used to describe the negotiation process as two people starting off from opposite sides of a totally dark room and groping their way towards each other until they meet. We use the image of the totally dark room because one side doesn't know where the limits are for the other side. The vendor doesn't know the maximum amount the purchaser will pay, and the purchaser doesn't know how little the vendor will sell for. (It's important to note here that often even the vendor doesn't know how low he will go in the sale. Many a vendor has gone into negotiations with a firm price in mind and wound up selling the property for an amount so low that he is astounded.)

In most cases, there is no such thing as a firm price. Sure, every once in a while you'll find a vendor who says he won't take a penny less than a certain amount and really means it. But these are the exceptions rather than the rule. And these properties aren't really for sale. In almost every case, a firmly priced property is an overpriced property. What you often see happen is that when the market moves up a bit, this kind of vendor moves up the price of his property, so that he is always "surfing" ahead of the market. The fact of the matter is that when this unmotivated seller acquires some motivation to sell, he will become like all the others. But until that happens, he's just cluttering up the marketplace.

I like to say that in any negotiation, the parties are only two dollars apart at any given time. The buyer has an amount that he won't surpass by even one dollar, and the seller has an amount that he won't drop even a dollar below. If you're the buyer, success is measured in how close you can get to the seller's amount. If you're the seller, success is measured in how far you can stay away from this amount. But all we're talking about is two dollars.

The Terms

There is a school of thought in real estate that says the price is not relevant. I know this flies in the face of everything you have been taught to believe, but it's true.

Let's take any small office building as an example. I am willing to buy it for $1 million more than its fair market value. Why? Because the terms I offer you are that I will give you nothing down and will pay no interest. I will keep 10 percent of the net income of the building and use the other 90 percent to reduce the mortgage owing. Do I care how long it takes to pay off the mortgage? No! Because eventually it will be paid off and I will own a building that cost me nothing.

In this scenario, the price meant nothing and the terms meant everything. Certainly, the terms have to make it as easy for you as possible, but bear in mind that it doesn't do you any good to grind out such a plum situation for yourself that the vendor can't live with it and kills the deal. This brings us to the concept — or should I say "fantasy"? — of the win/win situation.

I've said it before: every real estate deal is a zero-sum game. That means that what one person wins another person has to lose. Anything you leave on the table is a donation to the other side. So if you're in the game to make money, you should know what you're doing and what it's costing you.

The real secret to negotiating good terms is to ask a lot of questions (sound familiar?). You can't find out where the edges of the envelope are unless you press against them. The people who ask and explore wind up with better terms than the people who don't. Make up a set of rules for yourself and don't be swayed by what the vendor is asking for — you'll wind up meeting somewhere in the middle. If you don't ask, however, it's as if you're saying no for the vendor instead of having him say no to you. Ask and ask and ask. You'll be amazed at how often the answers surprise you.

This is a good place to talk about negotiating training. If you haven't had any, you should get yourself some. There are all kinds of good books and tapes and courses on negotiating. Buy some! It will be the smartest money you ever spend, and you will earn it back a thousand times over.

The Eleven Rules of Negotiation

1. It's okay to ask someone to do something you know he can't do — but don't insist on it.
2. Make sure you're negotiating with the decision-maker. If the person you're talking to doesn't have "the pencil," you're wasting your time.
3. Know what your deal-killer amounts and conditions are.
4. Have an idea of the other person's deal-killer amounts and conditions.
5. Know how much time you have to negotiate. Try to keep this a secret from the other side.
6. Find out how much time the other side has for negotiations, and be patient. Problems get solved one at a time.
7. There is always a hidden agenda. Find out what it is. Remember that you want to be a risk assessor, not a risk taker.
8. Any time you make a concession, get something for it in return. Always get something — no matter how small — when you give something.
9. The better the deal you make, the more important it is to let the other side save face. Negotiating is a contest, and the money is often secondary to the process itself.

10. Negotiate face to face. Lyndon Johnson once said, "If you're not looking in a man's eyes, you really don't know what he's going to do."
11. State your best case and then shut up and listen. The first one who speaks loses.

The Mortgage Amount

This is what will be left owing after you've paid whatever cash is necessary to do the deal. There are various ways to make this amount smaller. You can pay more up front, arrange for the owner to carry back some of the mortgage himself, or perhaps get a third party to provide some of the purchase price by trading some money for a mortgage.

But you don't always want the mortgage amount to be smaller — sometimes, in fact, you want it to be larger. If you've got a "nothing down" deal (or close to it), you may see that reflected in the price. And that's okay too!

The Mortgage Rate

This is sometimes just as important as the price. If you are arranging the mortgage through a bank, a credit union, or a trust company, then the rates are, within a certain range, going to be comparable and competitive. There is a lot of competition for that business, however, so the more you shop around, the better the deal you're going to make. Even if you know nothing about this when doing your first deal, you will have easily learned it by the time you've gone through the process once.

But banks, credit unions, and trust companies are just one source. There are all sorts of private players in the game as well, and here the goal posts get moved around a little bit. If you're going to deal with private money, you're going to have to know exactly what you're doing. For this, you'll want the services of a good mortgage broker. I'll deal with alternative financing sources in more detail in chapter 14.

As I said earlier, sometimes the best source of mortgage money is the seller himself. One thing they hardly ever teach in negotiation courses is a technique that I've used for years, and that is to ask the seller what he's going to do with the money he's going to get for the property. I can't count the number of vendors I've encountered who were bound and determined to sell for all cash and that was that. But when I asked what they were going to do with the money, they said they were going to invest it in mortgages. Well, you don't have to be a super-salesman to demonstrate to such a person that the smartest thing to do would be to invest in a property whose value they intimately understood.

When you are dealing with the vendor on the mortgage, you can do yourself some serious good because he doesn't have the institution's overhead. You won't be involved with loan fees and brokerage points, and he is as anxious to see the sale go through as you are. This is a genuine win/win situation. Vendors who put their money in the bank earn less interest than they can on a mortgage even 1 or 2 percent below market rate, and buyers can save the 1 or 2 percent negotiated. Some of the best deals you'll do will involve vendor take-back mortgages.

The Mortgage Term

This is the length of time it takes to pay off a mortgage, and it too is an important factor. The mortgage is measured not only in dollars but also in time. A mortgage, for example, can be amortized over twenty-five years but with a term of five years. That means your payment is calculated as if you were going to have twenty-five years to pay it off, but in five years you have a balloon payment for the total balance owing. Most of us think that the five-year term is only an interest-rate fixer. While that is true for the majority of residential mortgages, you must be aware that your financial institution is under no obligation to renew the mortgage. Many so-called investors will have a scenario where their rents are fixed but they speculate short on their mortgage term (in other words, they are gambling that they will be able to refinance at a more favourable rate). In my view, the best scenario is to fix your mortgage term to the length of the time you plan to keep your investment. If you don't do this, you are not only a real estate investor but also a speculator in interest rates.

There is a joke among real estate professionals that if you want the winter to pass quickly, you simply arrange for a mortgage with a balloon payment that comes due in the spring. Balloon payments aren't scary when you know what to expect, but the uninitiated are sometimes shocked when they experience one for the first time.

But balloon payments are also a technique that allows you to do a deal that would not normally be possible. Some entrepreneurs use this to push the present problem of not having enough money into the future on the theory that they will be able to solve the problem then. The seller isn't concerned, because the worst thing that will happen to him is that he will get his property back and he'll have it to sell all over again.

The point is that the mortgage term can be a tool or a trap — it all depends on how it's used.

The Source of the Money

This is usually the most important factor involved in the purchase of the property. (And here I'm talking about the source of the equity money, not the debt money.) I am reminded of a developer I knew who used to say, "I don't care how big a deal is. I don't care how complex a deal is. I don't care how risky a deal is. There ain't going to be any of *my* money in it!" I mention this only to illustrate that it is very possible to do deals using OPM — other people's money.

You'll find money in all sorts of places. There's your retirement fund. There are other people's retirement funds. There's the cash surrender value of your life insurance. Or you could get a loan from your father-in-law. The list is really endless. In fact, I believe that if you've got a good deal, you won't have to look too hard for the money — the money is looking for you.

The main thing to remember when using OPM is not to put too low a price on the deal. There is a factor that I call the arrogance of capital. People with money think that their money is more important than the deal itself, and therefore that they should command the lion's share. But the fact of the matter is that there is much more money looking for good deals than there are good deals that could use some money. The trick is knowing how to bring them together — or finding someone else who knows how. We'll talk more about this later.

Who Will Do What?

There are a variety of players involved in any deal. At a minimum, there is usually a vendor, a buyer, a lender, the person who is providing the OPM, real estate agents on both sides, a mortgage broker, accountants on both sides, and lawyers on both sides.

What you have to make sure you do is carefully and clearly outline what each party is going to do and when he or she is going to do it. This is particularly vital if you have a partner, joint venture or otherwise. Spell out your understanding in writing. It's also a good idea to create a critical path, so you have on paper the various components and time factors involved. If you do this, you know what you have to do to stay out of trouble, and more important, you have time enough to fix it when trouble does occur.

What you want to avoid is a situation where everybody assumes that somebody else is doing something and everybody knows about it except that somebody. Get the deal in writing and make sure that everyone who needs a copy has one.

Who Will Own What?

Here is where we cut up the pie. The very best time to decide who will own what is right at the beginning. People are a lot less greedy at the beginning of a deal than they are just before its culmination. As a result, you have a much better chance of putting a high price on your participation if you do it at the onset. Nothing loses value faster than services already performed.

I have a friend who says, "The only room people are going to give you at the table is whatever you can elbow for yourself." That may seem a bit cynical, but it is often true. And the time to do that "elbowing" is right at the beginning.

What about the Commission?

Sometimes the real estate commission is the most amount of cash that goes into a deal, yet it is the factor that is most often ignored during the negotiations. Be aware that the commission is not carved in stone — it is merely a number that somebody wrote on a piece of paper, and it takes but the stroke of a pen to cross it off and write a different number in its place. Real estate brokerage is a highly competitive business, and all commissions are open to negotiation.

You will be surprised what real estate agents will agree to once you start asking, especially when they view it as a choice between having some cash now or no cash later. (The broker has a time factor attached to his involvement, because his listing is for a finite period of time. If the property doesn't sell within that time, he has to renew the listing or lose it. This can be a powerful motivator.)

The commission can also be an excellent source of equity money if it's left in the deal for a time. All you have to do is ask the broker if he would like to become a kind of junior partner. Be creative, be imaginative, and don't be afraid to ask. I have met dozens of realtors who have taken back second mortgages to facilitate deals and actually built a substantial portfolio for themselves and their families. The real estate agent can see the value of having a bird in the hand as well as the next person.

THE LAST WORD

Remember that any deal involves only numbers on paper, and they can be moved around any which way. I guarantee you will find that people will always do what they perceive to be in their best interests. Your job is to shape their perceptions so that their best interests coincide with yours.

But timing is very important here. If the first thing you tell an agent is that she's going to have to leave her commission in the deal for three years, you're not likely to get much enthusiasm. But if you wait until just before closing, when the agent can feel and taste that commission, you'll probably get better results. I worked as a real estate agent, and I know that I'm not giving away any trade secrets here. This is all just common sense. The art of the deal is all about deciding who gets what. The more you learn and are able to apply what you learn, the better off you're going to be.

In Essence

> You don't get what you deserve — you get what you negotiate.
> The asking price is only where you start.
> In any negotiation, the parties are only two dollars apart — the one dollar below too little and the one dollar above too much.
> Ask and ask and ask. You'll be amazed how many times the answers will surprise you.

10

Buying

The customer can have anything that he is willing and able to pay for.

W ho should buy real estate? Well, that depends if we're talking about investment real estate and not just a place to live. Anyone who wants to get richer should buy investment real estate. There are ways to get richer faster, of course, and there are safer ways to get richer. If you go to Las Vegas and put your life's savings on the dice table, for example, you can double it in less than a minute — or reduce it to zero in the same span of time. Alternatively, you could put your money into government bonds and double it safely every fifteen to twenty years or so. But anyone with any sense of economic history will agree that the best bang for the investment buck is in real estate.

The longer you do it, the richer you're going to get, so start as young as you can. I have never had anyone say to me that they were sorry they'd started buying investment real estate so soon. Every person I've ever discussed it with said they wished they'd started sooner.

So we're agreed. We're going to start now. But what shall we buy? There are two basic categories: improved real estate and unimproved real estate. Do you want to buy a piece of unimproved real estate and wait for a city to grow up around it, or do you want to buy something already improved and rent it to somebody who will pay you for the use of it? It all depends on how busy you want to be.

Having said this, let me give you some advice that I think will be useful to you. If you're just starting out, buy something that is bite-size. Make it a sort of "earn while you learn" project. If you're already involved with real estate investing, then you should buy what you can afford. Don't forget the three ways to lose money in real estate: greed, ignorance, and bad luck. Don't let the greed get to you. Go a little slower and be a lot safer.

So where are we? You want to be richer, so you're going to buy some investment real estate and you're going to do it now. Next, you have to decide where to buy. If you're buying unimproved real estate you have the whole world to choose from, but if you're buying improved real estate you have to be very cognizant of geography. If you're a new investor, you would be well advised to buy as close to home as possible, especially if you're going to be doing the management your-self. Ideally, you should buy the property next door. That way, you don't have to go far when a pipe breaks on Sunday morning. The farther away your investment is, the more expensive and time-consuming it's going to be to manage.

If you think that your spouse or children make demands on your time, owning investment real estate will be a revelation to you. If you're at home with your family barbecuing on a summer's evening and your tenant phones that something has happened — let's say the hot-water tank has burst — you've got to deal with it right away. You can be going out the door with those theatre tickets in your hand when your tenant phones — this time, the tree in the backyard fell over and punched a hole in the roof — and you'll have to deal with it. That's why being in close proximity to your property is so important, especially when you're starting out.

The next question is when to buy. This time I don't mean the when of where you are in your life, but rather the when of where the real estate business is in any particular economic cycle. Should I plunge in? Should I bide my time? Are there better or worse times to buy, and how do I know which is which? Every factor in real estate investment translates into a financial impact on fair market value. Fair market value exists only in the present tense. Since we've talked about fair market value at other places in this book, suffice it to say here that if you buy at fair market value, the time for you to buy is *now*.

Sure, you can wait and times may get better, but that will be reflected in the price (i.e., you'll pay more). Also, times may get worse and stay that way for ages — then you could wind up waiting forever. The time to buy is always now!

THERE ARE NO GOOD OR BAD MARKETS, ONLY GOOD AND BAD DEALS

One of the reasons that real estate is better than other investment mediums is that it's certain. It also has a built-in investment discipline. If you've got a mortgage, you have to service that mortgage every month. It's a forced savings plan with the ultimate motivation: if you don't make that payment, the lender will come and take the property away from you.

But it's also important to be buying for the right reason. Any investment is, by definition, something that you expect to be able to resell at a profit. You also expect that the money you have invested will perform at least as well in this vehicle as it would in any other investment vehicle. Put another way, if there is something better to do with the money, then that's the thing to do with it.

The yield is also important. You can't get the optimum yield if you don't buy at fair or below market value. For the umpteenth time, let me reiterate that you're going to make your most money on the day you buy the property. And whatever you do, keep ego out of the equation. There's nothing more dangerous than a self-inflicted financial wound taken in the worship of ego (in other words, because you want to own the biggest or the best or you can put your name on the building). Save the ego for real estate that's for personal use. An investment should be about dollars alone.

The same thing goes for tax benefits. The tax benefit should be like the cherry on top of the sundae. You get it in addition to the investment property, but you do not buy because of it. Buying into a bad deal for its tax benefits is one of the more popular self-inflicted financial wounds. Never, ever look for tax shelters first. The deal *must* make sense by itself. More money is lost every year in real estate tax shelters than in any other real estate investment.

Okay, you know when to buy, where to buy, and why to buy, so now you need to decide how much property to buy. How far should you be stretching? Well, as we say when playing bridge, let's review the bidding. The more leverage you reach for, the more money you're going to make if you win. The flip side, of course, is that if you lose, that loss is exacerbated by the leverage. If you want to be absolutely safe from the risk involved in leverage, you have to buy for all cash. For most everybody, that means you'll never get into the game. Therefore, let's agree that there will be some sort of leverage involved — that is, there is going to be a mortgage. If you are just starting out, the best advice I can give you is to buy what you can afford. Especially at the beginning, you are better off buying too little than buying too much. You would also be wise to have a reserve for contingencies, such as vacancies or other emergencies.

When you first go out shopping in the marketplace, you're going to find it very confusing. Here is another instance where a written action plan is going to serve you well. You need to focus your attention on specific market segments. For optimum results, you should let as many people as possible know that you are a buyer. But at the same time, they should also be made aware of what your parameters are for type, price range, and terms. If you're not specific, you'll wind up wasting a lot of people's time — especially your own.

It won't take more than two or three well-placed real estate agents to keep you as busy as you want to be until you find something that fits your formula. If you also want to do some grave dancing with financially distressed property owners, you'll need to make contact with some mortgage brokers and loan officers and let them know that you're a potential buyer. Any loan officer with a problem loan has a situation that he's going to be anxious to correct.

Once you insinuate yourself into the marketplace, properties are going to start coming your way. If you have to choose between two or more, how are you going to go about making up your mind? A good method is to approach the problem from two separate perspectives: 1) reasons to buy it; and 2) reasons not to buy it. The first approach is much more important than the second. And it takes us back to one of our basic rules: It doesn't matter how many good deals you say no to as long as you don't say yes to something that could wipe out your capital. In other words, don't buy anything that is likely to get you into trouble.

Except for raw land, you have to manage whatever it is you buy. Things like single houses or condos do not generally need professional management, unless you've got a lot of them. That means you're going to have to do it yourself. When the pipe breaks, the tenant is going to call you and you're going to have to do something about it. When the tenant gives notice, you're the one who is going to have to get the place rented again. When the rent cheques stop coming in, you will have to attend to the eviction.

I'm not raising these points to discourage anyone; I'm just trying to present a balanced picture. You need to realize that anyone who is trying to sell you some real estate will extol the benefits without men-tioning the drawbacks. All those benefits come at a price, and you'll pay that price whether you know about it in advance or not. As usual, if you're well-informed, you'll find it easier to decide whether you want to pay that price or not.

WHEN YOU NEED ANSWERS . . .

The problem with any aspect of the buying process is that it's hard to know where to go for advice. Whatever you do, don't go to your lawyer or your accountant or your bank manager. If these people knew anything about buying real estate, they wouldn't be in their offices for you to talk to — they'd be out in the field. The person you do go to for advice is someone who is demonstrably a successful buyer of real estate.

Here are some random thoughts on sources of advice and elements of the buying process.

Bankers, Lenders, and Sources of Money

Don't be blindly loyal to your bank or financial institution. Shop around. You can expect to pay a slight premium if you're financing an investment property, however. Lenders are nervous people.

Accountants

Get advice on any tax ramifications before you buy. Be aware that the Tax Act now disallows all deductions on property for which you could have had no "reasonable expectation of profit." Talk about adding insult to injury. You lose money, and then they won't let you write it off.

Record-Keeping

I'd advise you to maintain separate paper streams and set up different bank accounts for each property. In this age of computer accounting programs, you may not feel you need this, but I still believe in the self-disciplining effect of having separate sets of books. No matter how hard it is or how little time you have, record-keeping is of vital importance.

Use of Equity

Once you've used up your borrowing power from your own income stream and starting asset base, link up the equity you have in existing properties. Wrap-around mortgages (i.e., mortgages that cover more than one property) can get you some of the elasticity you may need to buy that next piece of property. Remember that in inflationary times, leverage coupled with decisive action can make you very rich, very fast. But be careful — timing is vital. The farther out you walk on the leverage plank, the more difficult it can be to maintain your balance.

Vendor Take-Back Mortgage

As I noted earlier, the very best source of money can be the person you're buying the property from. First, you don't have to convince him of the value of the property. Second, he doesn't have to charge you as much as conventional lenders because he doesn't have their overhead. Third, there's hardly anything else he can do with the money that will give him the same return with the same degree of safety.

Line of Credit in Credit Cards

If you line up all the credit available to you in your credit cards, it's probably an easy $50,000. If you can support the monthly payments, you can go out and buy a $250,000 property with that. With just a few hundred dollars in annual fees, you could easily expand that by another $50,000 in a line of credit. Just don't get silly. And treat this as a very short-term strategy, because those interest rates can kill you.

Abatement

On most "no money down" schemes, there is some form of abatement included as part of the deal. An abatement is just a sum of money the vendor gives back, or rebates, to the purchaser on closing. As the purchaser, you could ask for this money to cover deferred repairs and maintenance or needed renovations. Alternatively, you could use this money to cover negative cash flow and put off the needed work until the income from the property will pay for a loan to cover it.

Often, the abatement is simply a way to purchase a property with nothing down. Let's say you purchase a property for $100,000. You get the maximum first mortgage of $95,000. The $5,000 balance is cash from you. But on closing, the vendor gives you a $5,000 abatement. Result? No down payment. When used properly, this technique can mean a giant leap forward in your investment program.

Deferred Payments

This is another favourite "no money down" strategy. It works well when the vendor takes back a mortgage. Using the above example, let's say you negotiate a $100,000 sale price with a take-back mortgage of $95,000 and a down payment of $5,000 due in cash six months after closing. At the same time, you negotiate for your first mortgage payment to start in six months. If the property can be rented at $1,000 per month — well, you get the idea. This works best when a quality buyer (i.e., one with good credit) meets a well-off vendor in a tough market.

Positive Cash Flow

If you don't know where you're going to get the money to cover the cost of operating the building and servicing the mortgage, don't go any further. It doesn't all have to come from the building itself, but it does all have to come from somewhere. And you have to know where that somewhere is before you buy. That's how you stay out of trouble, particularly when you buy out of town or in a market cycle that is flat or turning down. If your expectation of capital gain is a few years off, you *must* have cash flow.

View and Inspect

I've said it in a hundred places and in a dozen different ways, but here it comes again: you make the most money on the day you buy the property. Much of this money is in the price you pay and the terms you negotiate, but you can't know what price to pay and what terms to negotiate until you personally view and inspect the property. If you don't know what to look for, spend $200 and take along an expert to tell you what you need to know.

The Staying Power Fund

Nothing in life is predictable. You can't make a list of contingencies, because a contingency is something that isn't on the list. Start a fund to cover any emergencies that occur. In fact, this could be an excellent place for the abatement monies.

THE LAST WORD

When you're in the buying mode, you are king. Everybody in the entire real estate industry is working for you. But you are a buyer only as long as you're shopping and have those "buying bucks" in your pocket. Once you've made the transaction, you are merely a potential seller.

The buying posture is always powerful, and you should take full advantage of it. Any opportunities that you don't exploit are wasted. They are money thrown away.

◇

In Essence

◇ The ideal time to start is as soon as possible.

◇ The farther away your investment is, the more expensive and time-consuming it's going to be to manage.

> The farther out you walk on the leverage plank, the more difficult it is to keep your balance.

11

The Reality
of the Realty
Marketplace

Human kind / cannot bear very much reality.
— *T. S. ELIOT, "MURDER IN THE CATHEDRAL"*

The realty marketplace is a place of hard work where there are no free lunches and lots of competition. Is it as easy as it looks from the outside? Of course not. What you see from the outside is a duck gliding effortlessly through the water. But underneath the waves, those webbed feet are going like blazes. And that's exactly what this business is all about.

Think of what it took you to learn whatever it is you know about the business you're in. First, there was probably some schooling. Then there might have been an apprenticeship or a journeyman phase. And finally, there was all the on-the-job education, the learning experience that brought you to where you are now in your profession. Now consider what would happen if someone without any of your training or any of your experiences came along and tried to start doing your job from the word go. Would that person be successful? Of course not. There would be a lot of mistakes and a lot of learning along the way.

Don't expect the realty business to be any different. Skill and experience are as valuable here as they are anywhere else — with the added complication that any mistakes you make can be disastrously expensive. It's all a matter of odds and probabilities — you are rewarded (or punished) according to the risks you take. Out-and-out risk-taking is what you have to avoid. But to understand which risks to take and when to take them, you have to know how to assess them correctly. That is why you want to be a risk assessor first and a risk taker second.

Now, if people are not going to serve the apprenticeship and equip themselves with the knowledge they need, then what should they do? In a word: nothing. They should leave their money in the bank. They should let some bank or trust company manage their portfolio along very conservative guidelines. The results will be a little disappointing, but they will probably survive.

You don't have to be a Rhodes Scholar to conclude that if people are going to play in the game without having the necessary knowledge, they had better learn to link up with someone who does have the knowledge and whose interests don't conflict with theirs. In other words, they are going to have to hire some experts, or they may as well send all their money to their favourite charity and be done with it.

EXCUSES, EXCUSES, EXCUSES

So now we come to the place where we get all the reasons why you can't do the work that needs to be done. I'm too busy. I don't have the time. I'm this, that, and the other. Sure you are. But are you willing to lose money? Of course not! Yet that's what you're describing. And that's one of the reasons that I shout from the hilltops the importance of a written personal action plan. When you actually put your action plan in writing, you will find out if you're too busy to be playing the game. If you are, you must either drop out altogether or rearrange your priorities so that you do have the time to learn what must be learned.

As I just suggested, the first thing you have to do is learn how to assess risk. As soon as you've done that, you've got to decide what your own personal tolerance for risk is. This is a fluid condition, so you must be sure to keep reviewing and repositioning yourself. We change as we age, for example. The risks you will take when you're single and thirty are different from the risks you'll take as a married forty-five-year-old with three kids. And the risks you'll take at sixty, with most of your working years behind you, are different again.

Of course, your tolerance level isn't the only thing that changes as you age. In fact, most everything is different — patience, stamina, energy level, and so on. Your priorities also change. You constantly have to decide what's important to you because you're going to have to pay a price for everything you do. If you're married, you have to make these decisions in concert with your partner. You're both going to reap the benefits or pay the price, so the decisions involved should include both parties.

IT'S A CRUEL WORLD OUT THERE

If you really want to be successful, you have to teach yourself just how unforgiving the world is. The person you're buying property from cares only about himself. You didn't exist in his life before he met you, and you will cease to exist for him the minute he cashes your cheque. The same can be said of the buyer when you're the one selling the property. And the lender, if there's one involved, is even less concerned. Sure, he wishes you well so you will be able to repay his loan without causing him any trouble, but he did not enter into the transaction with the idea of taking any chances. As far as he's concerned, your relationship is about money and nothing else.

You need to know what your personal guarantee means before you put pen to paper. (It means that in any default situation, you are it!) Understanding the harsh realities of life in advance could just possibly make all the difference in the world.

I think misconceptions are what make the world seem so cruel. You know the kind I mean. "I can trust him — he has my best interests at heart." Or, "The brochure says I'll earn 24 percent on my investment, so it must be true." There are all kinds of misconceptions in this business. One of the most common is that if you just let enough people know that you are in the market for a bargain, one will be presented to you as soon as it comes along.

Not a day goes by without somebody saying to me, "Ozzie, when you see a good deal, give me a call and I'll buy it." Of course I will! Why wouldn't I? I certainly wouldn't buy it myself, or give it to one of my children, an in-law, or a close friend. No, I'm going to give it to you, a total stranger. Come on now!

If you're not out in the marketplace every day, all you are going to get are the leftovers. For one thing, bargains are not all that plentiful. Sure, they do come along from time to time, but then they go to the person who finds them. The trick in panning for gold is not just to get rid of the sand, but also to keep panning all the time. That way, you have a chance when a nugget does come along.

The formula is a simple one. If you work hard, spend a lot of time in the marketplace, *and* are lucky, you will get whatever share of the bargains that amount of talent and effort and luck warrants. If you lessen any one of the components of the formula, your share will be reduced commensurably. (And just as an aside, you'll notice that the harder you work, the luckier you get.)

But the real key is your willingness to take action. I have seen numerous cases where two people are looking at the same piece of property. One person is smarter, richer, works harder to locate deals, and is superior to the other in absolutely every way except one — the other person is more willing to take action. He makes up his mind a day before the first person and winds up with the deal. It is extremely important for you to keep in mind the idea that in this game, you get what you get because you're willing to take action. None of the sifting and comparing and analyzing means anything without the action.

SPECIALIZATION IS THE SECRET WEAPON

I can hear you now. But, Ozzie, with so many other buyers out there, can I really hope to compete effectively? Well, this is a good point. There is a lot of competition out there. And in all probability, at least half of them are going to be smarter than you, work harder than you, and outpace you in every category imaginable. Given that, how can you possibly hope to succeed? The answer is simple. If you're persistent, you will succeed. You just have to be consistently persistent.

And your secret weapon here is specialization. Real estate, like most any other field you can think of, has grown more complex in recent years. It is no longer possible to be a Renaissance man. There is simply no way you can cover the entire spectrum. What you should want to do instead is specialize in one or two areas. That way, you are going to optimize your chances for success.

So which areas should you choose? Well, that's up to you — urban, rural, single-family homes, apartment buildings. Choose whatever strikes your fancy. The only problem with specialization is that the field you choose may be attractive at the time you select it, but things could change a few years down the road. All of a sudden, single-family homes are choking the market, and all the money is being made in condos in some other city.

The graph goes up and the graph goes down, and I can't count the number of fortunes I've seen lost by people who couldn't let go and move to something else. The moral? Specialize but stay light on your feet and flexible.

THE LAST WORD

If you try to play in a game when you're not eligible, you will get eaten up. Most people run into problems in this area when they use their equity money to get into the deal and then rely on future financing to allow them to continue. The difficulty here is that they are approaching a three-dimensional problem with only two dimensions of awareness. And this is where eligibility comes in. If you get involved in a deal that is bigger than your financial capabilities, you may find that when you need new financing, no institution will lend you the money. Yes, you have a healthy debt/equity ratio. Yes, the property could cover the new mortgage. But if something happens to the cash flow of the property, you would not have the financial muscle to service a shortfall — and therefore, as far as the lender is concerned, you are not eligible for the loan.

When this happens, it triggers the whole domino effect of having to go to other sources for more expensive money or having to take in partners. Each time you do this, your position in the deal gets smaller and smaller and the distance between you and the return of your equity grows. If you want to avoid this particular reality, make sure that you're eligible for the size and type of deal you go into.

And finally, remember that the face of the marketplace is always changing. You have to keep up with the trends. Yesterday's knowledge and experience are good only if you use them as a base to build on today.

In Essence

> The realty marketplace is a lot tougher than it looks from the outside.

> If you're too busy to play the game properly, you should probably drop out altogether.

> The person you're buying property from cares only about himself. He'll forget about you the moment he cashes your cheque.

◇ If you're not in the marketplace every day, all you're going to get is what's left over.

◇ Stay light on your feet and flexible. Change is the only constant.

12

The
Resale

An investment is an investment only if you have a good chance of selling for a profit in the future.

The time to think about the resale of the property is before you buy it. You should have a clear idea of what you want to achieve and how you intend to achieve it when the time comes to sell. Those investors who make the most money on the day they buy do so because that's when they think about the resale.

It's not enough to throw yourself into an investment and then look for a soft spot to land later. You can do all right that way, of course, but what I'm talking about here is how to optimize and maximize your investment. Before you buy a property, you may, for example, want to consider just how you're going to take and hold the title. You may want to sit with your taxman and calculate how much you expect to make and how the title should be held so as to minimize the taxes. If you have some risky business activities in other areas of your business life, you may want the proceeds in the event of a sale to be shielded from any possible lawsuit and attachment. In a case like that, you should consider holding the property in a corporation, giving it to your spouse or your children to hold, or some combination or permutation thereof. All of this must be considered, decided, and acted on before you buy the property — it's too late after.

THE TIME/MONEY/PSYCHOLOGY EQUATION

The exit strategy should take into account any time, money, or psychological concerns. First, consider the time factor. How long do you intend to keep the property? There are all kinds of investment postures possible here. Some people think of their investment portfolio as a black hole — once something goes in, it never comes out. These people, whom I like to call keepers, buy a property intending to pass it from parent to child and so on *ad infinitum*.

Some people — the flippers — take the other extreme. They buy a property (preferably with a long closing period) with the sole intention of reselling it before they have to take title to it — ideally, later on the same day. And then there is everyone in between, the so-called normal investors. These are the people who want to hit a particular benchmark and then exit the investment. You need to know at the outset what kind of player you are and how long you intend to hold your property. No one approach is best — it's strictly a matter of different strokes for different folks.

But what happens if you're not thinking in terms of time? Well, many people decide to get out of an investment for financial reasons. Let's say, for example, that your investment approach is to acquire property with a leverage factor of 75/25 (i.e., you would put down 25 percent and the rest would be mortgage). In addition, you have decided that you never want to have an equity position of more than 50 percent in any given property. If you have bought a property for $100,000 (with $25,000 down), it would be time for you to sell when the value of that property rises to more than $150,000. Then you would take your $75,000 and buy a new property for $300,000.

In a case like this, reaching your benchmark could take more than ten years (if the market is slow) or less than ten months (if the property is rezoned a week after you buy it, let's say). You simply have to know in advance what your objectives are so you will know when to act. And the time to decide on these objectives is before you acquire the property.

The third factor of our equation — psychology — is the most subjective, and therefore the most difficult to determine. Your personal psychology keeps changing throughout your life. You might be greedier at twenty-five than you are at fifty or seventy-five. Certainly, your tolerance for risk lessens as you age. On the other hand, your patience generally increases. You must be constantly assessing and re-assessing any psychological factors that have an impact on your investment decisions.

And try to remember that none of the components of our equation exists in a vacuum. Each one has an impact on the other two.

WHAT HAPPENS WHEN THERE ARE OTHER PEOPLE INVOLVED?

An exit strategy is much simpler to devise when you have only yourself to consider. When you start adding more people to the mix, it gets complicated. If you're married, for example, you have to take into consideration the psychology and personal needs of your spouse.

And things only get more complex and harder to control once you get outside of the spousal association. If you're in a partnership, you're most likely in a "majority rules" situation. Often, you'll find yourself making compromises in a partnership that you wouldn't have to make as an individual. One way around this is to decide on some possible exit strategies before you even enter the partnership (in other words, much as you would do when purchasing property as an individual). You want to make sure, for example, that there are buy/sell and arbitration agreements in place in case of irreconcilable differences. The poet Robert Frost said it best: "Good fences make good neighbours." It is a simple matter of writing down *all* the eventualities you can think of — partner dies, partner needs money, partner doesn't do his part, partner brings in another partner, and so on — before the joining of hands, minds, and money.

The magnitude of the problems you can get into if you don't go through these steps is mind-boggling. For example, let's say that two families buy a holiday condo with the understanding that they'll "use it together." But what does that mean? Who gets Christmas and Easter? Who cuts the grass, does the dishes, makes the beds, and vacuums? What if one family is sloppy and the other isn't? What about pets? What about subleasing to outsiders? Can one family sell its half for whatever it can get, or does the other family get to buy it back at the original price? A hundred questions asked beforehand will make for a smooth partnership. Indeed, I have seen a lot of misery caused by little items that weren't covered. But that's why you need to go through this kind of analysis before you buy — so you can make the good deals better and identify the bad ones before it's too late.

So are partnerships bad? Of course not. But all partnerships that lack a clear, clean, itemized partnership agreement are flawed and can create a lot of unhappiness. On the other hand, carefully planned partnerships, I believe, have a good chance for success. I once owned a large yacht with three other partners, for example. Everyone said we couldn't make it work, but we did. However, our agreement covered *everything*. We all knew what the expectations, the rewards, and the recourse for non-compliance were. Thus we were able to enjoy a much larger yacht than any one of us could have afforded on his own. These kinds of partnership agreements are especially important when it comes to real estate partnerships.

WHEN IT'S TIME TO SELL

Remember that the very definition of an investment is something that you have a good chance of selling for a profit at some point in the future. If there is only a moderate chance of this happening, then we slip from an investment to a gamble. If there is absolutely no chance, I don't know what to call it — perhaps a tax loss that isn't complicated by the possibility of profit?

Of course, the fact that a secondary market, or a proven secondary market, doesn't exist in the present doesn't mean that one will not develop in the future. But that uncertainty has to have a dollar value attached to it, and that dollar value should be subtracted from the purchase value. Yet most purchasers don't go through the steps of this kind of analysis.

Still, let's say that you did everything right and time has passed and the property's value went up or down or stayed the same. You are now motivated, within the framework of your time/money/psychology equation, to sell the property. The next step is to analyze the methods that you're going to use to do this.

When I get ready to sell a piece of property, the first thing I do is look around for a real estate agent to handle the sale. Generally speaking, I use different kinds of agents for buying and selling. When I want to buy, I want an investment-oriented agent. I want that agent to understand that I am looking for a deal. I want that agent to be a person who will be scanning the market for the kind of motivated seller who will make possible the deal I want. That agent will be looking for divorces, foreclosures, mortgages in default, an estate turning an inheritance into cash, or any other kind of situation that might motivate a seller to take less than the current market value. In short, I — like all buyers — want the best price possible. If someone is going to buy a property for less than its current market value, I want that person to be me.

When I sell a property, by contrast, the agent has to understand different things. If I'm buying, I want to get within one dollar of the minimum that the seller will accept. If I'm selling, I want to get within one dollar of the maximum that the purchaser will pay. This is not as simple as it appears. Every seller wants as much as possible for his or her property, but I know from experience that overpricing that property is like taking it off the market. This is why it is so important to have an agent who is attuned to the market — to a degree, I am going to use his knowledge to arrive at my selling price.

Once I have selected an agent, I get him to prepare a written market evaluation. This evaluation will tell me the price he thinks he can get for the property. It should include nine comparables — three that have sold, three that are currently on the market, and three that have expired. I'll then take a day and look at those nine properties. I want to know whether the agent used the right comparables, and by the end of the day I should feel confident that the information he gave me is current and accurate. Once I'm comfortable with the dollar figure, I'll give him the listing on the basis of that price. But I will make sure at this point that he understands the rules by which I expect both of us to play. I want him to show me the action plan he will use to market my property. All other agents in the neighbourhood *must* receive information on the property immediately. (You may think your agent will sell the property, but in fact 78 percent of the time an agent from another company will sell it.) I want a weekly report, even if there is nothing to report. When the property is shown, I want to know the reaction of the people viewing it. Did they think the price was too high? Was the property too small? What did they say?

I make the agent understand that he's not supposed to try to beat my price down. If you want him to convey to prospective customers that this property is not a good prospect for a low-ball offer, you must first convince him of that. He will reflect your attitude and position, as he understands them, to every buyer with whom he comes in contact. That is why it's so important to program him.

Impress on him that you do not want to be snowed under with a blizzard of offers. The two of you have agreed on what the price is going to be, and all you're interested in considering are offers that meet your price and terms. Remember that he has been trained to bring you all offers, no matter what they are. You have to help him overcome this conditioning.

Your agent will be much more effective once he concludes that the price is firm, and that he's going to have to come close to it if he's going to make any money. I say "close to it" because, let's face it, you're going to have to let the buyer get in a few licks. Very few people can find it in their hearts to pay list price for a piece of property. You almost always have to throw them a bone at the end — but it doesn't have to be a big one.

Before you can play chicken with buyers, however, you have to be very attuned to the market. You have to know, almost to the dollar, what your property is worth as of that particular day. Fortunately, it's easy to know when you're wrong. If you're way too low, you'll be swamped with offers; if you're way too high, you'll find out what the word "lonely" really means. Accuracy is key here — so that's another reason to choose your agent carefully.

I know from a lifetime of experience that all the agent wants is for there to be a transaction. If there's a transaction, the agent will get a commission. If there is no transaction and the listing expires, he gets nothing. Let's look at the numbers to see what this really means. Say we have a $200,000 listing and the commission is 5 percent. If the property sells for $200,000, the agent gets $10,000. If the agent persuades me to take $180,000, then he gets $9,000. No question it's less money, but he gets it for sure and also diffuses the danger of the listing expiring. If you were the agent, what would you do?

My point is that the agent's agenda is not the same as the seller's. Human nature dictates that he serve his own self-interest. That's why you have to manage the agent very carefully if you want to maximize your results.

ONCE THE WORD IS OUT

Because I believe so strongly in the effectiveness of a written action plan, I require one of any agent to whom I give a listing. I want him to tell me in writing exactly what he is going to do for me as long as he has the listing. In addition to this, I require that he check in with me on a regular basis. When he calls, I expect a report on what new advertising has been done. If it is print advertising, I want a faxed copy of the ad. If it is electronic media, I want an audio- or videotape of the spot. If it's on the Internet, I want a copy e-mailed to me.

Next, I want to know how many people called about the ad. I want to know how many people viewed the property, and what their reactions were. This is not just idle curiosity — I need information like this if I'm going to make informed decisions. I may, for instance, want to change something about the deal, such as the price. I may even want to change the agent.

Okay, let's say you're doing everything right and the agent brings you a potential buyer. This is where you get to use all those negotiating skills that you acquired by dint of hard work and long hours of study. And of course, you know by now that the first rule of negotiating is that whoever is the least emotionally involved has the advantage. You have to project the image of someone who is totally without anxiety about this property. If you're selling, you want to convince the buyer that if you don't get your price, you'll just hang on to the property for three or four generations until some sensible investor is willing to pay what it's worth. As soon as there is the tiniest hint of blood in the water, the sharks will start circling.

By sending out the right messages about your strengths and keeping all your weaknesses to yourself, you'll be able to weed out all the investors who think like you. You're not going to be able to make a deal with someone who plays the game the same way you do. What you want to get is your share of the good buyers — and hopefully someone else's share as well! To do this, you have to approach the market with the right product at the right price using the right agent.

◈

In Essence

◇ The time to think about the resale of the property is before you buy it.

◇ Good fences make good neighbours. Partnerships that lack a clear, itemized agreement can cause a lot of unhappiness.

> If there is only a moderate chance of selling a property for profit in the future, it slips from an investment to a gamble.

◇ Choose your agent carefully. You have to manage him if you want to maximize your results.

◇ Broadcast your strengths and keep your weaknesses a secret.

13

Scams
and Shams

*The secret of selling is to find out what people already want
— and show them how what you've got will help them get it.*

This was one of the toughest chapters to write, because there are literally thousands of shams and scams to choose from. And unfortunately, human nature being what it is, there are literally thousands upon thousands of naive souls willing to take the bait. Why are so many of us so easily taken in? Well, it is one of the universal truths of life that, with the exception of truly remarkable creatures like Mother Teresa and Albert Schweitzer, we would all like to be rich. Indeed, we are conditioned by our upbringing and by observing the world around us to believe that richer is better. Besides, being rich will prevent you from being poor. Now that one *is* a universal truth.

This desire for gain is the first ingredient in any recipe for a successful scam. The second ingredient is often another belief that we take in with our mother's milk: real estate is a good way to get rich. Almost all of us have good feelings about real estate. Sure, there have been some complications here and there, but overall real estate is perceived as being a good investment bet. Finally, you add to these two ingredients the *pièce de résistance*, the man in the expensive suit with the gold Rolex who says, "I know how to solve the secrets of the cosmos. Subordinate your judgement to mine, and I will make you as rich as you want to be!"

Remember the quotation we opened the chapter with? That's why the equation works so well. People *already* want to be rich. They *already* believe in real estate. When someone comes along and sings a seductive song, they're like putty in his hands. It's a mystery to those of us who can't carry the tune, but it's easy for those who can. And it's a very simple step for the victims. Instead of making all those numerous individual judgements about the safety and viability of an investment, all the victim has to do is make the single judgement that the other person is honest and knows what he's doing. Once this conclusion has been reached, this particular universe will unfold the way it inevitably must: the victim will hand over the money and the con man will spend it.

LITTLE MONEY IS EASIER TO CON

There are basically two kinds of real estate shams. The first of these is the one-on-one scam, where a single piece of property is sold to a single investor. These are usually smaller deals. Then there are the development projects, where several investors are brought together to do a project of larger proportions. This second category rarely involves deals that are one on one. Instead, these scams are usually structured as syndications or limited partnerships or some other grouping of people in a single investment or a related series of investments.

For some reason that is difficult to explain, people are more willing to suspend their critical judgement when they are in with a group than when they are by themselves. Maybe it has something to do with the herd instinct or with some atavistic feeling that there is safety in numbers. Regardless, scam artists take full advantage of this fact.

Scam artists also like to bring together a bunch of small investors for a big project because smaller investors generally don't have the time, resources, or knowledge to recognize a scam for what it is. As one real estate wag once said, "Big money has a mind of its own. Little money doesn't have any mind at all."

If you're a big investor and you have a million dollars to invest in a project, you're going to examine it with a microscope before you go into it. You're going to have your lawyer and your accountant take a look at it. In fact, you're going to bring in whatever experts you need to examine everything with a fine-tooth comb. Because of the size of the investment, you're willing to spend a few thousand dollars to examine it, even if you wind up walking away.

On the other hand, if you're someone with only a few thousand dollars to invest, you are not likely to be as knowledgeable or as sophisticated as the man with the million dollars. And the size of your investment doesn't leave you the room to hire lawyers and accountants to examine it for you. Because he can't justify spending that kind of money on an investigation, the smaller investor often finds it's easier and feels it's cheaper to take everything on faith. In the end, unfortunately, it usually turns out to be anything but cheap.

For the perpetrator, there's another important reason why a group of small investors is preferable, and that is that as the project goes along, no one individual feels he has the right to say anything negative. Therefore, there's not going to be anywhere near the level of examination or interference that could come from one single large investor.

A BRIEF HISTORY OF SCAMS

"Florida swampland" is a phrase that has become a part of our everyday language. In effect, it refers to any worthless, overpriced piece of land that will never have any value. For generations, wily con men sold swampland in Florida to any gullible investors they could find. In other areas of the country, their cohorts were selling off pieces of the desert as prime Arizona real estate and arid scrubland in Death Valley as California farmland. There just doesn't seem to be any limit to the gullibility of people. One story claims that in California, land speculators would tie oranges to the Joshua trees (a kind of large cactus) and then sell the land to new arrivals as orange groves. In New York, con artists famously sold off pieces of the Brooklyn Bridge!

Of course, all these are examples of distance making the heart grow fonder. Do you think those pioneering con men sold Florida swampland to Floridians? How many Phoenix residents do you think bought acreage out in the Arizona desert for more money than property was selling for inside the city limits? Did the people in Beverley Hills overpay for desert scrubland simply because it was a three-hour drive from Los Angeles? Of course not! Anyone who was close enough to take a look at the property would know immediately that no one in his right mind should buy it. That's why the scammers sell the Florida stuff to Californians, the Arizona stuff to Floridians, and the California stuff to New Yorkers. Anything they have left over they sell to Canadians.

There have always been these kinds of scams going on, but the practice didn't develop into an art form until the late 1930s and early 1940s. These were the years when the regulatory agencies started getting serious about monitoring the stock market. With the heat turned up, a lot of sharp operators realized that they could take all the tricks they used selling worthless securities and use them in the real estate arena. Without even missing a beat, the former stock pros became real estate experts, printed up a new batch of business cards, and kept on doing business as before.

Of course, it was easy for them to make the transition because the principles are exactly the same. You see, the fact of the matter is that you can't cheat an honest man. Why? Because an honest man knows that there is no such thing as getting something for nothing. Greed and the desire to get away with something are what make most people vulnerable to being conned. If an investor doesn't have even the tiniest spark of larceny in his heart, he can't be cheated. The bigger the spark, the easier the con.

Why is greed so dangerous? Because it makes us act in foolish ways. People who have spent a lifetime learning whatever it is that they do for a living will take all that experience, knowledge, and good judgement and set them aside without even a second thought. Having known someone for all of an hour, they will decide to put their trust in him and then will proceed to hand over their life's savings. It is truly amazing!

These same people then think that the government should come and rescue them from their own incompetence. In fact, almost every time some project crashes and burns, you'll hear one of the victims sadly saying, "I thought the government had laws against this sort of thing. How could the authorities allow people to do this?" And of course, when people think that the government is looking after them, they feel they don't have to look after themselves.

Strangely enough, the government itself thinks that it is looking after people. Government agencies will tell you that they require the companies they regulate to make "full and true disclosure," and it's true. If you don't believe me, sit down with any real estate prospectus or offering memorandum and read it from cover to cover. If you pay attention, you will see that it says the project is risky. It will tell you there is an element of danger. It will stress that there is no guarantee. Yet the overall effect of this bureaucratic overkill is that those few people who do read the offering documents are anesthetized by all the legalese and wind up ignoring the whole thing.

SEPARATING THE WHEAT FROM THE CHAFF

The danger is that all deals start out the same way. Generally, the person heading the deal falls into one of three categories: honest and capable, honest but inept, or dishonest and corrupt. Unfortunately, everyone looks the same at the start. They all have the same approach, make the same claims and projections, and seem safe and trustworthy. (Anyone who didn't make the investor feel safe wouldn't do anyone any harm because he'd never get anyone's money.)

Ironically, I don't believe that the really dangerous person is the dishonest one. If you've learned anything from this book, you will examine him closely enough that you will never give him any money. And of course, the honest and capable person is the one who will really make you rich. No, I believe the most dangerous person is the one who is honest yet inept.

This person, because of his powers of persuasion, gathers together millions of dollars and then tries to take part in a game that he should only be watching from the sidelines. What usually happens is that he joins bigger and bigger games with more and more projects. Eventually, his need for cash to cover his overhead leads him into one non-viable project too many, and his canoe goes over the waterfall. That's the end of that.

Because the end result is the same as in a premeditated scam, people who were burned by an honest yet inept speculator often think they were cheated. But they're wrong. In fact, the person leading the deal usually winds up losing more than his clients. In effect, he, in an effort to keep the deal afloat, goes down like the captain of a sinking ship.

The investor, however, needs to believe that he was cheated. Somehow we believe that making an investment that failed because of bad luck is our fault, but that it's someone else's fault if we put ourselves into a situation where we can be cheated. Therefore, it follows that if I lost money, I must have been cheated — it certainly couldn't be anything *I* had any control over.

In cases like these, we have to remember that although the motivations of the people running the deal are different, the end result is exactly the same. You can't insulate yourself from bad luck, unfortunately. If you get into a deal that runs into bad luck, you're going to lose. But you can avoid bad deals, and you do that by asking the right questions and walking away if you don't get the right answers. Let's take one example.

SCAMS AND SHAMS — 125

I look in the paper and see an ad that says, "Come to the ABC Hotel at the corner of Juice and Spruce on Wednesday evening at 7:30 p.m. and John Jones will tell you how you can get rich with no risk." Right away, I should ask myself the following questions:

1. Why are these people doing this?
2. What is their track record?
3. What is the probability for success for a company that markets investment situations this way?

And the answers I should give myself are these:

1. Almost no successful real estate developers acquire their investment capital this way. They are doing this because they can't get capital from any other sources.
2. Companies like these almost never have a verifiable successful track record.
3. More than 90 percent of the companies that raise money this way wind up going broke and costing their investors all their money.

But let's say that you are a persistent little devil and you get past the first three questions. You decide to attend the seminar. The man with the gold Rolex has the stage and a microphone, and he tells you his remarkable story. The questions you should ask *him* are:

1. Why are you people doing this?
2. What is your track record?
3. What is the probability for success for a company that markets investment situations this way?

And the answers you will most likely get from him are these:

1. We love the little people. We are doing this for them because we have all the money we will ever need.

2. Our methods are so revolutionary that no one has ever used them before. But we have been outstandingly successful in practically every other form of human endeavour, so don't worry.
3. See above.

By now, any reasonable person would have given up on this situation, but if you look in the dictionary under the word "persistence," there is a picture of you. So when this guy phones you in about a week, you make an appointment and go to his office. While you're there, he shows you the particulars of a specific investment and you ask the same questions and he gives you the same answers. But now he is also stressing how safe and secure you are, because you are going to be protected by a *mortgage!* And that magic word casts a spell over you. Unfortunately, you don't think to examine this closely enough to determine if there is, in fact, enough value in the property to give you the protection you need. You give him all your money, and eventually you lose it.

So what is my point? Well, simply that the problem isn't so much with how one regards the answers, but instead is that the person who refuses to ask the questions is going to get stung.

By the way, it may interest you to know that even after you lose all your money, that's probably not the end of it. Let's say you claimed certain tax deductions that the tax people don't agree with, for example. They'll want that money, and they'll want it with interest and perhaps even some penalties. Or say the company you invested with paid you interest for a year or two before going bankrupt. You'll want to regard that as a partial repayment of your capital, but the tax people will regard it as interest earned and they'll be expecting back taxes with interest. Talk about adding insult to injury!

What anyone who has ever experienced one of these deals wishes is that he could turn the clock back to the day he first invested and take a different turn in the road. But staying out of trouble is easier than that. Do not get embroiled in deals like these in the first place! If you find one being presented to you, ask the right questions and listen to the answers.

WHAT IF IT'S ALREADY TOO LATE?

Now, let's say that you are in one of these deals right now and it hasn't gone over the cliff yet. Things are still rolling along. What should you do? My advice is to go and make so much fuss and so much noise and be such a bother that they will buy you out to get rid of you. Get them to pay you off with the next investor's money. Of course, you could be the straw that breaks the camel's back and triggers the collapse of the whole deal. But if you don't try to get your money back, you're going to lose it for sure. You may as well at least make the attempt.

What about after the collapse? Here, sadly, is where people throw good money and effort after bad. You pick up the paper one day and see that the company can't make its interest payments or pay its bills any more, and that the regulators have issued a cease-and-desist order. Your knee-jerk reaction is to go to a lawyer, complain to the government, or join a committee of other unhappy investors. But none of these will give you any satisfaction. Indeed, everything you try to do after the fact will probably be a total waste of time. You should just learn from the experience and get on with your life.

THE LAST WORD

All of this seems so simple, so why is it that every few months we read about more people losing their life's savings? Don't people ever learn? Sure, they do. But the public memory is relatively short, and so there is a never-ending supply of people who have to learn the hard way. It is the old, old story of the sardine and the shark. There is no power on earth that is going to keep these two apart — though the problem is not the strengths of the shark, but the weaknesses of the sardine.

If you know of someone who is contemplating this kind of investment and you want to do him a favour, give him this chapter to read.

◇

In Essence

◇ At its heart, any scam involves one person subordinating his judgement to another's. Everything after that is just arranging the details.

> Big money has a mind of its own. Little money doesn't have any mind at all.

◇ If an investor doesn't have even the tiniest spark of larceny in his heart, he can't be cheated. The bigger the spark, the easier the con.

◇ Good deals, bad deals, and dishonest deals all start out the same way. The trick is in learning to separate the wheat from the chaff.

> You can't insulate yourself from bad luck, but you can avoid bad deals. You do that by asking the right questions and walking away if you don't get the right answers.

◇ Once you've been burned, your best recourse is to learn from the experience and get on with your life.

14

Financing

Money is like muck, not good except it be spread.

— *FRANCIS BACON*

Okay, you've found a piece of real estate you want to buy, so now you need to decide how you will pay for it. Obviously, the very best way to do it is with no financing at all. Pay cash — but only if you have the cash and don't have anything better to do with it. This kind of deal would be called 100 percent equity with no financing, and it doesn't happen very often. In fact, most of us will go a lifetime without ever meeting anyone who has done a deal this way.

If you can't, or won't, finance the deal with your own money, there are two alternatives. You can fund that part of it that is not covered by your own money with equity financing or you can fund it with debt financing. What's the difference? Equity doesn't have to be paid back, but someone else will own a piece of the deal. Debt has to be paid back.

If you have the choice, you will usually elect to bring in equity financing when there is more risk involved than you would like. If you're comfortable with the level of risk, you'll probably elect to use debt financing. A good rule of thumb is to use more OPM (other people's money) when the risk is high. If the deal has as much chance of success as wildcatting for oil does, the OPM should be as close to 100 percent as you can get it. (Note that debt financing is always totally OPM unless you are borrowing from your own or your spouse's RRSP.)

When deciding just how much OPM to use, you have to ask yourself how greedy you are — or better yet, how greedy you should be. If you're not greedy enough, you'll be leaving chips on the table for someone else. If you're too greedy, you may do yourself an injury. Everyone has to decide his comfort level for himself.

SOURCES OF FINANCING

Okay, so where are we now? You're going to buy a piece of property and you know that you're not going to pay cash, so that means you're going to have some equity and some debt. You also know that the equity is going to be made up of either your money or someone else's money, or some combination of the two. The rest of the purchase price is going to be debt financing.

At this point, you have to learn what debt/equity ratio you're going to be involved with. If you put 20 percent down and finance 80 percent, that gives you an 80/20 debt/equity ratio. This isn't something you will decide, however; it will be decided by the lender. Every lender has guidelines for debt/equity ratio, and you will not be allowed to put in less than the guidelines recommend for your particular case (though of course you can put in more). Be aware of the leverage factor. People who get into trouble most often do so by reaching for too much leverage. It's better by far to be conservative and be able to survive the bad times.

So where can you go to get the money you need? Well, here are the main sources of financing, from the cheapest to the most expensive.

A Family Member

The first source — and everybody's favourite — is your father-in-law (or any other well-heeled relative). This is the easiest and best source primarily because the price is always right. And if you run into problems, you're going to get more leniency here than anywhere else.

Pensions and RRSPs

The next best source is your pension plan or self-directed RRSP. If your pension plan allows you to invest in mortgages on real estate, you can sometimes structure things so that you can get at the money for your own mortgage. You'll be able to pay yourself the minimum interest the tax people allow (or more, if it suits your purpose), and if you run into problems, you can be as lenient with yourself as you like.

You can also grant your own mortgage from your RRSP. The plan must be self-directed, however, and usually this scheme makes sense only if you have a minimum of $50,000 in your plan.

Canada Mortgage and Housing Corporation

The next source is CMHC. This is a good source for funding investment real estate, and it is usually a terrific source of financing if you're buying a home to live in. If it's a first home you're buying, it can be even better, since the rates will be the lowest you can find at arm's length. CMHC doesn't actually lend you the money, but it insures the loans that approved lenders can make to you. This makes it a simple matter to shop for the loan. This is really the only source, other than the vendor take-back mortgage, that will allow you to get 95 percent financing. But it costs you — the insurance fee is substantial.

Other Agencies

Because the government is always being pressured to do something about creating reasonable housing opportunities, you can sometimes look there for the money you need. But much depends on the kind of housing you're considering and the state of the money marketplace at that particular time.

Foreign governments are usually not a good source if you're investing outside the country. You're not a voter or a taxpayer, and your other assets (if the government wants to get at them) are usually in another country. All in all, you are not a very attractive prospect.

Vendor Take-Back

If you can convince the person who is selling you the property to carry the mortgage, or part of it, this is called a vendor take-back. If the vendor doesn't need the cash right away, it's a good investment. In fact, if there is a sufficient down payment, it's a well-secured investment at a better rate than the bank will give on the deposit end. For the vendor, the worst thing that can happen is that the property will come back into his possession.

Even if you cannot make a large down payment, vendors will often provide first or even second mortgages. This is the source of most "no down payment" deals, deals that offer abatements, and deferred payment structures. It can be the most innovative source of financing.

Corporate and Private Lenders

If none of the above sources pans out, you have to start going to strangers — that is, banks and credit unions. Now you're talking to people who don't want to run any risks, which is why they grant only 75 percent maximum first mortgages. With banks and credit unions, the debt/equity requirements and all the terms and conditions are going to be more stringent, and the rates are going to be WTTWB (whatever the traffic will bear).

After the banks and credit unions, we come to mortgage companies, insurance companies, and trust companies. They are just as careful as the banks, but their rates are going to be a titch higher. When dealing in this arena, you would be well advised to use the services of a mortgage broker. Your mortgage broker can make sure that your application package is in the form it should be and that you're approaching the right source. This is an area where it pays to have a professional; the do-it-yourselfer just doesn't fare well.

Next in line are the private lenders, and this is where it starts to get tough. The private lenders take the deals that the banks and the mortgage companies said no to. You should approach them only as a last resort. Their rates are higher; their fees are higher; and they charge higher points. And if you get into trouble, you're in a lot more danger than you would be with a bank or a mortgage company.

Finally, we're left with what I call the Yellow Pages lenders. These are the people who advertise a very low rate to bring the customers in, but hit them with stratospheric fees and points when the deal starts to come together. They usually do business in the area of refinancing. Once a borrower has got into trouble on an existing loan, he will sort of work his way down the financial food chain until he has to go hat in hand to these lenders. A distressing number of these loans wind up going into foreclosure, with all the attendant pain and anguish. Naturally, you should avoid this category if you possibly can.

Refinancing and Development Financing

Refinancing can be easier or harder than securing the original loan, depending on what has happened with the real estate market, your property, and the financial markets in the intervening years. If you can, you're better off refinancing with your existing lender. But again, shop the market and make the best deal you possibly can.

Development financing is a different art form. For this, you're definitely going to need the services of a mortgage broker. With development financing, lenders care more about the track record of the person behind the deal than they do about the security in the real estate itself.

Development financing is not as chancy for the lender as it may first appear. That's because of something called a hold-back. Usually, the lender appoints a quantity surveyor, whose job it is to measure how much of the development is done and how much it will cost to complete the part that is as yet unfinished. The lender will then hold back the amount of money that would be required to finish the project. That way, if you get struck by that proverbial bolt of lightning, the lender will only be out of pocket for the flowers he sends to your funeral. Then he'll get someone else to finish the project so he can get paid.

Personal Guarantees

There is a real estate philosophy that says, "A personal guarantor is a jackass with a fountain pen." I think I agree. Almost without exception, if a deal requires a personal guarantee, you shouldn't be in it. I can't count the number of people I know who have been wiped out because they signed a personal guarantee. And I mean really wiped out — not just the business assets, but the house, the cars, the bank accounts, everything!

Having said that, I realize that there are all sorts of situations where you have to sign a personal guarantee if you want to sit in on the game. I won't argue with anyone who decides to do that — so long as that person knows in advance what can be involved.

Let's consider the example of Christopher Hemmeter. At the age of fifty-eight, he had amassed a fortune of $200 million. But when he got involved in developing a gambling casino in New Orleans, he went bankrupt. His bankruptcy statement said that he had $720,000 in assets and $87 million in liabilities. The $200 million was all gone. Because he'd signed personal guarantees, he lost his homes, his cars, his bank accounts, and his customized airplane! When a reporter asked him in an interview if he would ever go into a deal of that kind again, Hemmeter said, "I'm an entrepreneur. An entrepreneur takes chances. Of course I'd do it again!"

The lesson here is that if the game is big enough, you could be betting the whole store. If that's the kind of a player you are, that's all right. You just don't want to be taken by surprise.

A Word about the Internet

The Internet is going to have a huge effect on how mortgage business will be done in the future. Every bank, trust company, and most mortgage brokers are already on the Net. Soon, the old ways of obtaining a mortgage will be completely displaced by electronic technology. This will be especially true in the area of single homes.

Right now, the entire home-buying process grinds to a halt and everyone stands around and twiddles their thumbs for anywhere from three days to two weeks while mountains of paperwork are transported from point to point. The Internet is going to change all that. Indeed, the first part of the equation is already in place: the borrower has the ability to communicate electronically with any lenders who are anxious to do business. The second part of the equation will be a "scoring system." Credit checks will be done electronically and actual documents will be required only for the file. Preliminary approvals will be given where merited, and final approvals will be given after a full-scale document review.

So get yourself set for this modern era. Whether you're a buyer, seller, realtor, lawyer, or lender, you're going to have to understand the new ways of doing business.

SIXTEEN WAYS TO SAVE MONEY ON YOUR MORTGAGE

1. *Try not to take the mortgage just the way it comes off the shelf.* Mortgage concessions are negotiated in exactly the same way as any other business deal. The lender is going to present his standard package, which is really just his wish list. If you want special treatment, you're going to have to ask for it — and you'd better be prepared to sell the lender on why you deserve it. If you're a long-time customer who has his RRSP and his business and personal accounts with the institution, point this out. All this will help you to negotiate the best rate.

2. *The better you look, the better the deal you're going to get.* For the lender, there is almost always some discretionary leeway from the posted rates, and this leeway can be as much as 1.5 percent. It's up to you to make the lender want to use that discretion. Most of the time, all you have to do is ask. The rule of thumb is that you can knock off three-quarters of a percent for any mortgage up to three years and a full percent for a mortgage over that. Bigger discounts are available at times. If the lender perceives that you're a shopper and that you know what you're doing, he will give you what you want just to keep you from going somewhere else. If you're a heavy-weight borrower, you should be able to squeeze out another quarter or half a percent simply because you've got some muscle. One thing is for sure: you won't get anything if you don't ask.

3. *Ask for a longer grace period.* In our newsletter, we advise our subscribers to get pre-approved in writing. Most people take the verbal commitment seriously, but in an environment where interest rates are always changing, I don't believe it's worth much. *Get your pre-approval in writing.* Once you have it, you can make low, no-subject offers on the real estate you buy. Ask the lender to extend

the standard sixty-day grace period to ninety days. This extra time will help you in your negotiations.

4. *Make the lender believe that you will direct more business his way.* When you are asking for reductions and concessions, you are asking the lender to take less money. Sometimes you can sugar-coat this pill by making the lender believe that you are going to give his institution more business. If you're dealing with a bank, you could shift your other accounts over. This can sometimes make the difference between a yes and a no.

5. *Be prepared to put all your strengths on paper.* Lenders rarely rely on charisma and other such intangibles when making their decisions. The more often your strengths are delineated and reinforced, the better your chances of getting the loan and at least some of the concessions you're asking for.

6. *Give your contact person the tools needed to get you what you want.* The person you see and charm at the lender's place of business may just be an information taker. To facilitate your loan application, you should make sure this person has all the information the final decision-maker could possibly need. There are three principle factors that are going to be considered:
    a) Equity. You have to know in advance what debt/equity ratios the lender requires for the type of loan you're seeking, and you have to make sure that you have enough equity to qualify.
    b) Stability. Have you had a presence in the business community for some time? If you're self-employed, does your work history extend far enough to make you look good? If not, be prepared to explain why. Erratic work histories make lenders nervous.
    c) Cash flow. Is the lender going to be satisfied that in an emergency, there is enough money to service the loan?

7. *Give as much security as you can to get a more favourable debt/equity ratio.* You can dramatically increase the amount that will be advanced if you re-mortgage, co-guarantee, or cross-collateralize any other property you have. But do this only if you need to for a larger or better loan.

8. *Make as large a down payment as you can if it will make a difference in determining the rate.* Remember that you're going to be paying this for twenty-five years; those little fractions of a percent can translate into tens of thousands of dollars of extra payment. Take a minute and work out your deal. Often, people take out CMHC insurance even if they have 20 percent down (banks will lend only 75 percent). Yet they would be better off taking a 75 percent conventional loan from the bank, getting a small 5 percent second from either the vendor or another lender, and saving the large CMHC fee. CMHC fees run into several thousand dollars. Use the insurance only if you need to take out the full 95 percent loan.

9. *If your stability looks questionable because you've changed jobs recently, do something to make yourself look more reliable.* If you've changed jobs but otherwise have a long and uninterrupted work history, stress this with the lender. It's also a good idea to provide a concise explanation of the reasons for the change with all the other documentation.

   Also, before submitting any loan application, check with the credit bureau to see what it's saying about you. If there is something in your file that is incorrect, send in the appropriate documentation and get it corrected. You can also enter a narrative into your file to explain the extenuating circumstances behind any credit difficulties.

10. *If you're self-employed, get your accountant to help you with the numbers part of your application.* Lenders have a little more trouble with self-employed people than they do with regular wage earners. Self-employed people generally get paid more sporadically, and

thus are complex to evaluate. If your numbers come from an accountant, they will carry more weight with the lender.

11. *If you're dealing with a bank and you're uncertain of your standing, make your initial run at the manager rather than the mortgage officer.* The manager can make an immediate call on amounts, rates, and rate reductions. The mortgage officer almost always has to get permission.

12. *Take advantage of the "new customer" factor.* In markets where lenders are slugging it out for new customers, you can often score brownie points just by walking through the front door. But if the marketplace is crowded with borrowers, you'll do better where they know you. This is particularly important at renewal time. Do *not* automatically renew your mortgage with your existing bank. You can almost always get a better deal if you switch!

13. *Save money by shortening the amortization period.* Don't get locked into the mindset that the twenty-five-year loan is a concept carved in stone. My own favourite term is seventeen years. The amount you save is astounding! Let's say, for example, that you have a $100,000 loan amortized over twenty-five years with a payment of $861. The same loan carried over seventeen years at the same rate will require a payment of just $978, or an extra $117. That extra four dollars a day will save you — are you ready for this? — $82,656 in interest. If $117 a month is too much, do it for half and save $41,328.

14. *Check rates to the last minute.* Even if you are pre-approved and closing in a week, call your mortgage broker to check on the rates. Financial institutions like to match their funds (i.e., they don't like to have cash lying around and not working for them). Sometimes institutions will give a very favourable rate for fast closings and particular terms. It's worth checking.

15. *Try to renew your mortgage in U.S. presidential election years.* In the autumn of any election year, interest rates are traditionally at their lowest. A more cynical person than I am might suspect that politicians do this to butter up the voters. Is this possible?

16. *Avoid frills and thrills.* Many mortgage companies offer you the "thrill" of a toaster, a car wash, airline points, and other goodies. These are *never* better than getting your mortgage rate reduced. Think about it. On a $200,000 mortgage, a one percent reduction translates into $2,000 — and that's just in the first year! Now think about the term and multiply. Forget the frills — get the rate cut.

THE LAST WORD

Negotiating financing can be simple or complex. Before you even approach a lender, it's wise to get a handle on whatever policies the institution has for evaluating things like cash flow and payment ability. If you're too weak in these areas, you may need a co-signer.

Of course, everything I said about a guarantor being a jackass with a fountain pen goes double for co-signers. I would advise you never to be a co-signer unless you are getting paid as if you were investing the amount of cash for which you are co-signing. But if you need a co-signer, you'd better hope that person hasn't read this book.

If you're refused by one institution, don't be discouraged. Find out why, do what you can to rectify the problem, and then try again. If the institution says no again, go on to the next one. Different institutions give different weight to elements such as equity, stability, and cash flow. What flopped with one lender could fly with another. This is where the mortgage broker comes in handy. But if you're going to use a mortgage broker, use him from the beginning. If you've already shopped your deal all over town and everyone has said no, there isn't much a mortgage broker will be able to do for you.

Don't lose sight of the fact that attitude counts. Lending has a human side to it. If you're organized, courteous, and make a small effort to assist the loans officer, you'll often discover that he will bend over backwards to accommodate you if he can. In fact, a lot of mortgages are turned down just because the borrower makes a bad first impression. So comb your hair, dress like a business person, and have your paperwork in a tidy and organized form. In other words, try to make it easy for the loans officer to give you what you need.

Remember that you're going to live with this loan for a long time — so bargain hard. You get only one kick at this particular can.

In Essence

> If you want special treatment, you have to ask for it.
> Save money by shortening the amortization period. Seventeen years is my personal favourite.
> Time your mortgage renewal to coincide with U.S. presidential elections.
> If you're turned down by one institution, find out why, correct the problem (if you can), and try again.
> Do whatever you can to make it easier for the lender to give you what you're asking for.

15

Value

What is a cynic? A man who knows the price of everything, and the value of nothing.

— OSCAR WILDE

In real estate, there really are only four principle means of determining what the market value is: the replacement cost method, the return-on-investment method, the comparable method, and the cardiac method. In life, however, there is one additional overriding principle of value. I'll talk about each of these principles as you make your way through this chapter.

THE REPLACEMENT COST METHOD

This is a bricks-and-mortar approach where you separate the building from the land (you calculate the value of the land using the comparable method). Making allowances for the age of your original building, plus any wear and tear, you determine what it would cost to replace the building with another of the same size and quality. This gives you the value of the property itself (minus the land).

Lenders and insurance companies like to use this method. It is important for them to know what it would cost to replace a property if, as an example, it burned down tomorrow. This can become particularly critical in tough times, when so many borrowers would like to see their property burn down. But if you're using this method, it's important that you be equipped with all the relevant information.

Let me give you the example of a property I've been watching for years. This land, which had been occupied by a dry-cleaning plant for several decades, was eventually rezoned for high-rise residential development and purchased for that use. The purchaser, because he was buying with the intention of tearing down the building, was concerned only with the value of the land and the demolition costs. He thought that in comparing his property with similarly zoned properties in the neighbourhood, he had an accurate idea of the land's value. What he didn't know was that for about thirty years, the dry-cleaning plant had been dumping its chemicals into the ground the building sat on. The ground was so polluted that the new owner couldn't get a building permit until he'd cleaned it, which took about three years. So in this particular case, the replacement cost method was misleading and got him into serious trouble.

You can also get into trouble with the replacement cost method if you overbuild an area. If you are in a neighbourhood with $200,000 homes, for example, and you build a $500,000 home, you can use this method to tell you the *cost* of the improvement but not the *value*. The only way your home will have a value of $500,000 is if you find someone as crazy as you are to sell it to.

My point is that this method is very unreliable. Replacement costs have very little to do with the value a buyer will place on a property. In fact, the actual cost of the building doesn't generally interest the buyer at all; she's concerned only with the price. If the price is half of what it cost, so much the better.

THE RETURN-ON-INVESTMENT METHOD

You use this method not for single-family homes but for income-producing property. An income-producing property is a business or an apartment building, and these sell on the basis of how much you can make on the money you have invested in relation to the risks you have to run.

Let's take as an example any apartment building. You can separate the land and evaluate that by the comparable method, then evaluate the building by the replacement cost method. But the real value is going to be determined by how much money can be made from running that apartment building, and that evaluation has to be done at a moment frozen in time. You can't say, "Well, we are in an inflationary economy and every year the value is going to go up X number of dollars, and so my price is going to be calculated with that increase factored into it." That won't work, I'm afraid, because you can't charge tomorrow's price today. If you want tomorrow's price, you'll have to keep the property until tomorrow.

The value of any income-producing property can be based only on what it will yield today. If you try to charge more, people will take their money elsewhere.

THE COMPARABLE METHOD

This method involves comparing a piece of real estate with other real estate that is similar, and it is the most widely used method. The accepted wisdom is that comparable pieces of real estate (i.e., those that are recent and similar) have the same value.

For instance, let's say you have a home with three bedrooms, two bathrooms, and a full basement sitting on a large lot in a residential neighbourhood. One block over there is another one just like it, and a block from that there is another one just like the first two. It's possible they were all built from the same set of plans and maybe even by the same builder.

If the second and third homes each sold last week for $100,000, we would probably assume that the value of the first house was the same. And as long as we're talking comparables, we would be right. But let's suppose that house number one is right beside the city dump and the others are not. That's going to mean that they are not really comparable, right? The word "similar" was not properly satisfied, because the houses were similar in look and size but not location. Every positive and negative factor has to have a dollar amount attached to it, and that amount has to be either added to or subtracted from the value.

"Recent" can also be a relative term. In a fast-rising market, it can mean comparable sales from last week; in a slow one, it may mean comparables from six months ago. In the case of out of the way or oddball properties that rarely sell, an acceptable "recent" comparable may be a year old. Generally, the freshest possible sales are used to compare the property.

You're probably getting sick of hearing this, but I want to stress again that in evaluating comparables, you can't tell anything by looking at statistics on paper or even by looking at a property from the outside. You've got to get inside, if you can. You have to know the whole story if you're going to draw an accurate comparison.

I know of one house that was used as a comparable in an evaluation and really shouldn't have been. The house was unusual because the owner had a very odd hobby — he raised foxes. Unfortunately, he kept his foxes inside the house, and the stench had permanently permeated the structure. You couldn't be in that house for more than a few seconds without your eyes tearing and your stomach doing flip-flops. Naturally, this house was priced about $30,000 less than it would have been if it weren't for the foxes, and yet it was being used as a comparable for other houses in that neighbourhood.

You have to make sure that you are comparing apples with apples.

THE CARDIAC METHOD

With the cardiac method, you stand in front of a property, put one hand over your heart, and say, "This property is worth X number of dollars. I can feel it right here in my heart!" It is, of course, the least accurate of the methods, but I never cease to be amazed by how many people actually use it.

The real point here is that you shouldn't allow emotion to enter into your thinking when you are determining value. If you encounter someone on the other side of a transaction who is using emotion and the numbers are in your favour, then by all means let it work to your advantage — just never let it work against you.

WHAT IS VALUE?

At the beginning of this chapter, I said I would introduce you to four methods of determining value and one principle that overrides them all. The principle is this: value does not exist in any physical, permanent way. Values change and move based on the perceptions of buyers and sellers in any given marketplace.

Thus value can be a very nebulous thing. In an earlier chapter, I already debunked the myth that interest rates drive market values. (If you believe you can make 30 percent on an investment, you do not care that you're paying a 15 percent interest rate.) And of course, one of the themes of this entire book is that you can put no stock in the "location, location, location" principle. Instead, it is the perceptions of buyers bidding for the same commodity that drive values higher (we all want it) or lower (where's the door?). Your biggest challenge is to overcome your emotions and take a reasoned approach. If you have your plan of action and understand your objectives, you will govern yourself accordingly. Emotions will be kept to a minimum.

When people talk about value, they sometimes refer to a "buyer's market" or a "seller's market." The seller's market is another myth. The buyer always sets the price. The only thing the seller can determine is if there's going to be a transaction or not. In fact, if there ever was a situation where the seller could name the price, that price would go through the roof. And of course, any time the seller moves his price to a point where it is more than buyers will pay, that property has, for all intents and purposes, been taken off the market.

You must also remember that all real estate values have to be calculated on the basis of what a property is worth today. You may have a theory of what is going to happen with trends and prices in the future, but that's a separate thing. You base the price at which you will either buy or sell a property on that property's value in the present.

Still, just because we say that your theories about future value are not part of determining the present value doesn't mean that they aren't a very important component in the process. Real estate is a commodity, and you can make a lot of money with practically no risk if you do it right. If you buy property because you have a theory about what's going to happen in the future and that theory turns out to be correct, you put yourself in position for an extra win. Of course, your success in this area will be determined by how much information you have and how well you interpret that information.

The dangerous thing about research is that it can be like animal tracks in the snow — they will tell you where the animal has been but not where it is going. Examining a trend's history will, in much the same way, tell you where the trend started but not where it will end up. Still, history does have a way of repeating itself — especially the bad parts. In real estate, it's particularly true that those who do not remember the mistakes of the past are condemned to repeat them.

We should know from personal experience that trends really do not go on forever. Positive growth is not necessarily a given. People don't keep coming into an area indefinitely. Inflation can't be depended upon to rise with the sun every morning. So never pay good money for some indistinct benefit in the future, and never let it be the reason you buy. Future benefit should be like the icing on a cake.

CAN VALUE BE ADDED?

As I've already said, the person whose opinion counts the most when it comes to value is the buyer, because he is the one who is going to set the price. There are two other potential players in the game, the seller and the end-user, but the main player is always the buyer. No matter how strongly the seller feels, only the buyer will ultimately determine if there is going to be a transaction. The end-user is really just another kind of buyer. His perception of value will determine what he will pay for the use of the property, and this in turn will tell the buyer what the property should be worth to him.

As I've said, value is not a static thing. It changes with the demand for the use of the property and also as the property depreciates with age or appreciates from inflation. However, there are things we can do to increase the value of real estate.

The first and easiest of these is to make changes of a purely cosmetic nature. Cleaning and maintaining a property can add to its value. We can also make physical changes that are a little more serious. We can, for example, paint and remodel (good), or we can get really serious and start moving walls and putting on additions (bad). The extreme version of this is when we knock the building down and put up something new in its place (it depends). But you should always be aware that once you reach the point of diminishing returns, you are merely adding to the cost, not the value.

You have to be careful to put a dollar in only if you're confident that you're going to be able to get more than a dollar out. And the extra amount you get out has to be worth the time, effort, energy, and risk that you assume. If there is something better you could do with the money, that's what you should do with it.

There are ways to add to the value of property without making physical changes. You can alter the terms, for instance, so that you make it easier for someone else to own. This means you're really adding to the value of the money you have invested in the property rather than to the value of the property itself, but who cares? It all adds to the bottom line.

Sometimes taking different factors and marrying them allows you to create value. Let's take the example of a business that rents its premises. You decide to buy the business from the owner and the premises from the landlord. Now you're in a position to marry the goodwill of the business, which is intangible, to the value of the real estate, which is tangible. You will have created a new whole that is greater than the sum of the parts.

Sometimes you can attach to the property amenities that didn't exist before. I remember once hearing the story of an investor who bought a condo project that was in dire straits. The developer had built a nice product, but he got caught in a shift in the market and went broke because he couldn't sell the units and the lender wouldn't give him any more time. When the lender tried to sell the units, he didn't have any more luck than the developer. The investor optioned the property under very favourable terms and then put a creative plan into action. He owned an athletic club a half a block away from the project, and he attached a membership to each condo. If you bought in, you got a two-year membership in the athletic club for free. In a very short time, he had sold the entire project and made a pile of money.

Of course, these are just a few examples from a list that is never-ending. Like the investor I describe above, you must try to come up with some creative ways of adding value. Think of the myriad things you can do with some simple trees, for example. You can harvest them and sell the timber. You can cut them down and open up views or create extra parking. You can plant them to provide shade and privacy. Just watch out for the environmentalists. Taking an axe to a tree can mean you will never be lonely again. You will have enough nature lovers around you to provide you with company for a lifetime.

Sometimes there are hidden factors that can add to (or detract from) the value of a property. Encroachments, easements, and zoning limitations can all have an impact. For example, I know of a property that abutted a large tract of undeveloped land. Because of a misinterpretation of boundaries, the owner of this property had built a very expensive swimming pool and cabana on the undeveloped tract. A purchaser for the tract, when researching the property, noticed this encroachment, so he bought the land and then told the pool owner he could either purchase an easement or remove his pool. The pool owner paid an amount that was just a few dollars less than what it would have cost him to remove the pool and cabana and rebuild them on his own property. He came out of the whole experience sadder, poorer, and wiser.

This was a case where someone knew something that someone else didn't know, saw how it could be used to create value, and then acted on it. Let me give you another example. There was a large abandoned vineyard on the edge of the high desert in California. The original owner had gone broke trying to make wine that no one wanted to drink. For decades, the land was vacant because no one could figure out a use for it. Everyone had forgotten that there were four abandoned wells, each one close to 200 metres deep. In fact, it turned out that there was an unlimited amount of water available from these wells because the property sat on a huge underground lake.

One wise investor found out about this underground lake and the four wells by reviewing old county water records. He bought the property for practically nothing, then drew up a plan to plant eucalyptus trees and sell the wood for firewood. (Eucalyptus trees grow about four metres a year, especially if they have all the water they need.) He then turned around and resold the property with that plan in place. In other words, he used the wells, which weren't even a selling feature, to practically double the price of the land, thus demonstrating that demand for use is the most important factor in determining value.

So what do these examples tell us? You have to stay light on your mental feet. Nothing ever stays the same, but sometimes things change for the better and sometimes they change for the worse. Whoever gets the relevant information first and interprets it correctly is going to have the advantage. And because nothing ever stays the same, there is no such thing as security. Given this, you may ask, where is the line between investing and gambling? Tough question. I suppose that if you're interpreting data and acting accordingly, you're investing. If you're using a crystal ball and depending on luck, you're gambling.

One thing is for sure: If you are going to gamble on changes, you must do it for the long term. If you try to do it for the short term, you'll find you have a better chance with lottery tickets.

THE LAST WORD

Will Rogers once said, "You better buy some land — they're not making any more of it." Strictly speaking, that isn't true. Whenever land changes from unusable to usable or from low density to high density, it is as if new land has been created. And this isn't unheard of. In fact, all kinds of changes can happen — highways get built, land comes out of the agricultural freeze, ferries are established, land that is recreational becomes urban, zoning restrictions get changed. But all of this moves with glacial slowness. If you play this game, you use a calendar, not a stopwatch.

And of course, different skills, when combined with a specific piece of real estate, can add value. A sheer cliff face may be of no value to most people, but it could be the perfect place for a bungee-jumping teacher or a hang-gliding instructor to open a school. Ideally, you want to be the middleman who buys this cliffside from someone who hasn't clicked to its possible uses and sells it to someone who has.

Of course, the best-case scenario is finding that person whose subjective opinion of the value of a property causes him to either sell for too little or buy for too much. Fortunately for us, there are as many examples of this as there are people on the earth. Just remember that value, like beauty, is more often in the eye of the beholder.

In Essence

- > There are four methods of determining value, but each one has its drawbacks. Value is not a physical, permanent thing, so it can be difficult to calculate.
- ◇ There is no such thing as a seller's market. The buyer always determines the selling price.
- ◇ You must base the price at which you will either buy or sell a property on that property's value in the present.
- > When attempting to add value to a property, you must ensure that you put a dollar in only if you're confident that you're going to be able to get more than a dollar out.
- ◇ You must not let emotion enter into your thinking when you are calculating value.
- ◇ Demand for use is the most important factor in determining value.

16

Sharks and Flippers

Anytime there's a real estate transaction, somebody is probably making a mistake. When a shark or a flipper makes a transaction, somebody is making a big *mistake!*

In this chapter, we're going to talk about sharks, the predators who swim through the real estate waters looking for an opportunity to feed. They prey on the weak and the unwary, and when they find such a person, they gobble him up. But sharks are not bad people — they are simply opportunists who take advantage of other people's misfortune. They know how to avail themselves of opportunities when they arise.

We are also going to talk about flippers, those real estate investors who look for opportunities to buy and resell very quickly. In both cases, we're dealing with real estate practitioners who are constantly sifting through the inventory that is available until they find someone who is either ignorant or in trouble, or both.

As I've observed before, real estate is a zero-sum game — in other words, what one person wins, another one loses. In short-term real estate transactions, this is especially true. If the potential is there for a quick resale at a higher price, the seller has, in effect, lost out on whatever the buyer gains. Of course, it's not that any additional value was created when the property changed hands. No, that value was always there. What we're measuring now is the awareness of that value and the property owner's ability to hang on to it. This is the milieu of the shark and the flipper.

You will hear people say, "Oh, you can be a shark only when times are very bad." Or they may say, "You can be a flipper only when there's an active market with a high inflationary factor." As with so many things in life, this is both true and not true. Yes, bad times make it easier for the shark and good times make it easier for the flipper, but both can also ply their trade in all kinds of markets and all kinds of conditions.

Market conditions are always relative. If you have a mortgage you can't pay, for example, it doesn't matter if you're in the best market ever. In essence, the quality of the market simply tells us how many transactions make up the averages. And sharks and flippers don't deal in averages — they deal in *exceptions!*

Exceptions, of course, happen in all kinds of markets. The trick is finding them, recognizing them, and taking action before someone else does. It may seem to you that the shark is out there looking to prosper from someone else's misery, but is he really just taking advantage of a golden opportunity? Is the flipper an opportunist who will exploit someone else's ignorance for his own personal gain, or is he a wily investor who recognizes potential profit when he sees it? You have to ask yourself where you draw the line between morals and business. It's different for each individual person.

If you're an idealist, I suppose you might come across someone a day away from being foreclosed on and say, "No, I cannot bring myself to profit from the misfortune of one of my fellow human beings. I will go on to something else, where I can pay fair market value and still be able to face myself in the mirror each morning." If you have philanthropic tendencies, you might find someone who has his property on the market for less than fair market value and say, "Hold on a minute, you are way too far under the market. I insist that you let me pay you fair market value so I will be able to sleep with a clear conscience." I have no argument with either view, and I'm not recommending any particular philosophy. All I'm saying is that if you play in this game, know where the goal posts are.

JUST WHEN YOU THOUGHT IT WAS SAFE TO GO BACK IN THE WATER

The shark will always be able to find customers, whether times are good or bad. He especially likes properties that come available because of illnesses, deaths, divorces, job transfers, business reversals, job losses, or bankruptcies. But people who got too greedy, too sleepy, or too stupid are also grist for his mill. Bad times make the soup a little thicker, to be sure, but the opportunities are always there.

For the flipper, the good times that come with a rising market and rapidly climbing inflation give him the most opportunities. But even in a flat market with no inflation, he can find deals. He has to work a little harder and wait a little longer, of course, but the deals are still there. The flipper does have to be aware of what I like to call the bigger fool theory, however. You've probably heard people use this theory before. "I am a big fool to enter into this deal," they say, "but an even bigger fool will come along and buy me out at a profit." This is all well and good until we come to the last fool in the line. He's the one who winds up with no one to sell to.

In a rising, inflationary market, there is a tendency to jump on the conveyor belt at any price because you believe a bigger fool will come along and take you out at a profit. This is where you need options and subject clauses to give you a way out if the music stops and you're without a chair.

Sometimes you will find an investor who is either a shark or a flipper, depending on which way the wind is blowing in the marketplace. In fact, the two types of investors are not so far apart. They both have an uncanny ability to recognize the signs, interpret them correctly, and act quickly and without hesitation. Those three characteristics are the toughest things to learn about real estate investing.

When I think about this aspect of the business, I picture an old-time miner standing at a sluice box, shovelling sand and gravel in and letting the water wash out everything but the nuggets. The more sand and gravel he processes, the more nuggets he's going to wind up with.

In many ways, we are like that miner. Our challenge is to get the most sand and gravel into the sluice box in the most efficient manner possible. In our case, though, the sand and gravel are pieces of information that we have to process quickly and interpret correctly. So how do we do this? Well, most of the information can be found in the databases and multiple listings of realtors. To take full advantage, you should find yourself an unbiased, independent real estate advisory service or a professional realtor and let them provide you with the information you need. For instance, my weekly *Jurock's Facts by Fax* service features five to ten deals each week. These are sent to us by banks (foreclosures), owners (those who want to get out), and realtors (who are looking for quick sales). Since we have a very large subscriber/investor base and charge no commission, this service is becoming very popular. Call 1-800-691-1183 for a *free* one-month subscription and see for yourself.

I read about one shark/flipper who had an interesting *modus operandi*. He'd developed a technique that allowed him to go up the down staircase. Rather than trying to associate with the most successful agent in a company, he would walk into an office and talk to whoever had "floor duty" for that shift. His theory was that the really big producers probably already had pet clients who were going to get the first look at any good opportunities that came along. But newer, less productive agents had all the time in the world to provide him with the information he needed and do the research that he wanted done.

You certainly don't have to be shy. If you identify yourself as someone who will act decisively when you see something that fits your formula, you will have no shortage of agents who want to work for you. But you have to make sure that they understand your parameters. Almost all the trouble that ever arises between clients and agents comes from a breakdown in communication. This breakdown is *always* the fault of the client, because he hasn't communicated the parameters to the agent in a form that he understands and believes.

Finding the right agent is key, and this is especially easy to do when there is a downturn in the market. Anytime you pick up the paper and see that real estate offices are closing because of a drop in the volume of business, you know that there are hundreds of agents who will do almost anything to pick up a new client. And once you've actually done a deal with an agent, you will own him for life.

CASH IS KING

You will make your best deals when you can buy for cash and sell for paper. You'll get the lowest prices and best terms and will move to the head of the line when you're buying for cash — particularly in a down market. And you will get the highest prices and best terms and will be the first choice of purchasers when you're selling for paper. I know a lot of people who make a business of this. Remember, for example, our Paper King in chapter 4? He bought for cash, sold for paper, and then, when he had amassed a small portfolio of paper, sold that paper and turned it back into cash.

If you're sharking or flipping, these techniques are going to make you as effective as it's possible to be. But this, of course, is possible only if you actually have the cash. If you don't, you can try to partner up with someone who does. If you have a good deal, you should have no trouble finding someone with cash to be your partner. Two of our newsletter subscribers, a young couple, went to Edmonton in the summer of 1997 and assembled a portfolio of $1.9 million in just nine months. All the properties they acquired were single-family homes (best for capital gain), all of them had basement suites (best return for properties bought with a low down payment), and none was bought with their own money!

How did they do this? They found willing investors in B.C. who wanted the play but not the work. These investors put up between $5,000 and $20,000 per property, and then the couple and the investors bought the property together. The couple did the legwork, found the deal and the tenants, and now manages the properties. Cash flows tops 15 percent, and in three predetermined years (remember that good joint-venture agreements spell everything out beforehand) they will sell and split the profits. Of course, here is where good timing really helps.

Robert Allan, the author of *Nothing Down*, used to boast that you could take away all his money and his credit cards, take him to any city in the U.S., give him a hundred dollars for expenses, and in seventy-two hours he would have bought at least one piece of property.

Now, you may not be any Robert Allan, but getting out in the field and taking action is still the most important part of the equation. And as I've said so many times before, one of the most important decisions you need to make is how far afield you want to go. The answer to this question all depends on what's happening in your own area. If times are good and the opportunities are available, you can do business in your own backyard. If times are tough and all the action is somewhere else, you may have to cast a wider net. But most of the successful sharks and flippers I've known have done their best business fairly close to home.

I know one very successful person who has a rule that he won't go more than three hours' driving time from his home. That way he can, at the very worst, go there and back in a single day. But your decision about distance will depend on the size of the deals you're doing and how much money you can make. Let's face it, if the price is right, you'll go to the dark side of the moon. If the price isn't right, you won't go across the street.

Another question you need to consider is when to keep and when to flip. This one's a toughie, so let me use an analogous situation to shine some light. I have a friend who, in his younger days, was a taxi driver. In fact, he was the best taxi driver in his city, and he consistently made more money than the other drivers did. His secret was a simple one. Taxi calls are dispatched from various zones of the city. They go on a first-come, first-served basis to the cabs that are booked into those zones. My friend knew from experience where the active zones were at various times of the day. "The zones of the city are like the squares on a chessboard," he explained. "I know where the other cabs are and I know where the calls are likely to originate. I never let my cab stand still if there was a chance to improve my position, and I never moved my cab if I was in the best possible place to be."

In other words, if there is something better you can do with the money, get rid of the property. If there isn't something better to do with the money, stay where you are. But remember to keep examining your position all the time, because the market is always changing. Nothing ever stays the same.

MAKE SURE YOU HAVE THE RIGHT TOOLS IN THE TOOL BOX

One of the most powerful tools sharks and flippers can use is the long closing. A long closing is like a free option. If you have sixty or ninety days to find a new buyer and effect your resale, you'll feel like the money fell from the sky. If you are fortunate enough to be able to write in some subject clauses that will allow you to get out of the deal without a loss, so much the better.

The powerful thing about subject clauses is that after sixty or ninety days, you can go to the vendor and say, "Look, I can't consummate this deal because my subject clause hasn't been satisfied. But if you give me a sixty- or ninety-day extension, I'm sure I can put this together." Then the vendor has to choose between sticking with the devil he knows, which is you, or going back on the open market and starting all over again. You'd be surprised how often — and how easily — those extensions are granted. After all the dust settles, you wind up having the equivalent of a six-month option for free.

So where do some of the most successful sharks and flippers find their deals? One place is at real estate auctions, where cash is really king. But to play this game, you need to have market knowledge, discipline, and patience if you want to avoid getting killed. If you lack even one of these qualities, they will hand you your head. You have to be able to go to an auction and sit there all night, bidding only up to your limit and no further. Often, you will go home empty-handed time after time until you get what you want.

Although in Canada auctions are relatively new, they have been around for centuries elsewhere. Generally, there are two kinds. One is driven by a developer who is trying to find a new way to market units. This kind you want to avoid, because the developer will not sell if he doesn't get his "reserved" price (thus there are few bargains to be had). The other auction is the type driven by financial institutions. This is where you want to be. The institutions want to clear out foreclosed developments so they can get the most cash back as soon as possible. Usually, all of the units, or at least a good portion, have no reserve (i.e., any price will get the unit).

Things to Remember about Auctions

1. *Auctions are never haphazard.* They are carefully coordinated and timed to create the maximum level of buying urgency. The idea isn't to give you a deal, but instead is to get the maximum possible return for the vendor/developer.

2. *Watch out for shills.* While no reputable auction house would do such

a thing, a disreputable one might employ a shill to bid against a legitimate bidder and boost the final price.

3. *Do your due diligence beforehand.* Look at the units. Identify one or two you will bid on, and don't bid on anything else.

4. *Position yourself in the auctioneer's sightline.* If bids are made at the same time, tradition says the bidder closest to the auctioneer takes the deal.

5. *Auctions are a psychological game.* Do a head count when you arrive. If there are a lot of heads and not too much product, come in bold and strong right off the bat. If voice bids are allowed, jump right in instead of waiting for the auctioneer to prod the bids along. This will overawe the other bidders and allow you to scoop up a unit. A good auctioneer with a full room will actually encourage a "good buy" up front to get the crowd heated up. As the night goes on and the remaining bidders fight for dwindling product, people actually end up buying at more than market prices.

   If it is a cold and miserable night, however, and the auction room is half empty, you should consider the opposite strategy. Rather than roaring in, wait for the true buyers to spend their budgets and then make your move.

6. *Never go in without your finances ready.* Be prepared with a large enough deposit to hold your suite and a pre-approved mortgage to allow for a fast close.

7. *Make your bid in small increments.* If an auctioneer has bounced along in $10,000 increments and the bidding has slowed, offer a much smaller increase. Let's say, for instance, that the bidding has slowed at around $120,000. When the auctioneer asks if someone will bid $130,000, offer $121,000. Often that will become the final bid.

8. *Never forget that both types of auctions have only one objective: sell the units.* If the unit you pre-inspected didn't sell or your bid wasn't accepted, consider going back to the auctioneer immediately after the auction and offering the same price again. The auctioneer, after all, eats only what he kills. He will go to the developer to check, and it's possible that you will still get the unit at your price. I have seen this work very well if the auction was a disappointment. The frustrated developer might decide to wash his hands of the whole thing and let you have your unit for cheap.

SOME OTHER GOOD SOURCES FOR DEALS

When it comes to auctions, you never know when you're going to get lucky. People get tired, bored, and impatient, and all of the sudden it's the end of the auction and you're the only customer with the knowledge, cash, and wherewithal to do a deal. You can do yourself some serious good.

Generally speaking, I have seen better deals made at auctions (sometimes even those with reserved opening bids) than at foreclosures. Foreclosures appeal to the shark, but in most parts of Canada you have to be a very patient shark indeed. The foreclosure dance in this country is carefully choreographed to benefit the homeowner as much as possible.

If you are trying to find a foreclosure property, be patient and don't expect anything to be easy. The only successful sharks fishing the foreclosure waters are those who deal directly with the owner during the *order nisi* period (i.e., the grace period the owner is granted before he is foreclosed) and consummate a deal before it gets to court.

Despite all the press write-ups to the contrary, we see very, very few investors who are consistently successful in this particular area. The same goes for the much-touted "tax sales" you sometimes see advertised on late-night TV. Usually, the situations being talked up are in the U.S., where foreclosure and repossession laws are much tougher on sellers. In Canada, properties are rarely sold for taxes owing.

Land assemblies are another good area for the flipper. If there are several parcels involved, you can step in and get long options and advantageous subject clauses for above the fair market value of the individual parcels (i.e., by paying tomorrow's price today). When you've got it all together, the new whole is much greater than the sum of the previous parts. And if you were one of the parcel owners and someone came along and wanted to pay you more than your property was worth, wouldn't you consider such an offer? These kinds of assemblies are particularly effective if zoning has just changed or is about to change.

So whether you want to be a shark or a flipper — or both — your success is going to depend on your ability to gather accurate, up-to-date information, interpret it properly, and then act upon it expeditiously. It may sound easy, but it is as much an art form as it is a business. As with everything else, you should start small and build to where you want to be.

In Essence

- Sharks and flippers can both ply their trade in all kinds of markets and all kinds of conditions.
- Sharks and flippers don't deal in averages — they deal in exceptions.
- Finding the right agent is key, and this is especially easy to do when there is a downturn in the market.
- You will make your best deals when you buy for cash and sell for paper.
- If you're going to play the auction game, you need to have market knowledge, discipline, and patience.
- In Canada, we see very few investors who are consistently successful buying foreclosure properties. The foreclosure dance in this country is carefully choreographed to benefit the homeowner as much as possible.

17

Limited Partnerships, REITs, and Hotel-Condos

*Once upon a time there were three brothers. One of them
invested in REITs and syndications, another invested in
limited partnerships, and the third became a bull rider in
the rodeo. The first two always considered the third one to
be the sissy of the family.*

More properly, this chapter about limited partnerships, Real Estate
Investment Trusts (REITs), and condos operated as hotels should
be in a book about the stock market, because these activities have much
more to do with securities than they do with real estate. But we're going
to deal with them here because these investments involve the use of real
estate and they are sold as if they were real estate.

Any time you are a minority shareholder or a participant in a joint venture, you are in effect handing over your money to someone and saying, "Here you are. Take this money and do the best you can with it." Therefore, the factor that outweighs all others in the evaluation process is track record. Ask yourself if the guy who's going to be running the show has done this kind of thing before with investors who were satisfied with the outcome. The answer, if it isn't the right one, can save you all kinds of money. Mind you, you have to be willing to turn on your heel and walk away.

The odds are that if you make an investment without getting a satisfactory answer to that question, you're going to be sorry. Unfortunately, the sad fact of the matter is that most people don't even ask the question to begin with.

But that's enough of a preamble. Let's look at each of these investment vehicles in a little more detail.

THE LIMITED PARTNERSHIP AND SYNDICATION

There are two kinds of partnerships. A general partnership is one where all parties have unlimited joint and several liability. In a limited partnership, by contrast, the liability of passive participants can be limited to the amount they've contributed or agreed to contribute to the venture. Of course, within each of these broad categories there are numerous permutations and variations. There are limited partnerships where the lender participates, for example, and others where partners in property are secured by mortgage bonds. All varieties come with different tax structures, benefits, and pitfalls.

Unfortunately, most scams and shams are found in the area of limited partnerships. Because investors believe their potential losses are limited, they are sometimes less rigorous than they should be about examining a deal. This makes them easy prey for a good con artist. That is not to say that there are no good limited partnerships, of course. But you must be aware of the fact that a lot of fringe operators fish in these waters. To help you separate the wheat from the chaff, let's take a quick look at the bewildering array of partnerships and joint ventures — limited or otherwise.

Joint Ventures

Joint ventures encompass a broad range of relationships and structures, and they can mean vastly different things to different people. Still, most joint ventures fall into one of the following three categories.

1. *A single-purpose corporation that is owned jointly.* This is the simplest kind of joint venture. A one-time company is formed, with each participant a shareholder. There is limited liability for the participants (if the deal explodes, in other words, you won't lose your shirt in a lawsuit). This entity doesn't permit any flow-through of income or expense.

2. *A co-tenancy relationship where each party has an undivided co-ownership interest in the real estate.* Here the liability is separated — that is, one party isn't jointly and severally liable for the actions of the other. Income and expenses can be lifted out for tax purposes at the individual level rather than at the joint-venture level. This means the benefit accrues directly to you. Co-tenancies have no communal ownership; the intention is to share gross returns, not net income. They're often used in a situation where there's one passive and one active participant. They're also effective if one party provides land and/or financing and the other puts in the management or development expertise.

3. *A partnership formed for a single project.* In this case, participants jointly contribute money, property, knowledge, expertise, or other assets for a specific project. The agreement may include a right to a joint-property interest in the subject matter, a right of mutual control or management, or a right to participate in profits.

Several Questions You Should Ask before
Entering into Any Partnership Agreement

1. Who owns what, and what percentage does everybody have?
2. How much has each participant put in? If someone is putting in know-how instead of cash, how is the non-monetary contribution measured?
3. What is the financing of the deal? Recourse or non-recourse? Collateral security? Guarantees?
4. If something unexpected pops up, how will it be addressed?
5. What fees or compensations will be paid to the parties? (You must particularly ask this question if the deal is being marketed through the financial-planning community. I have seen dozens of limited partnerships that paid the financial planner 10 percent up front and his company a further 3 to 5 percent. Some front-end loads in deals sold between 1993 and 1999 were as high as 27 percent!)
6. When and how will the cash flow be distributed? This is really important. In some deals, there is no expectation of return for ten years and it says so right in the offering memorandum (which, of course, no one reads).
7. How do I get out? At what point can I sell? When will the partnership be wound down?
8. What happens if disaster strikes? What are the remedies in event of default? Will my interest be diluted? Can I be forced out, and if so, will it be at a discount? Can the other party make a default loan? If so, at what rate?
9. If everything refuses to break apart cleanly, how will the impasse or dispute be resolved? Is there a right of first refusal?

Don't be afraid to ask direct questions and make your own inquiries. Ask for financial statements and the names of prior business partners, then check them out. Most deals are killed not because one partner was cheating the other, but because needed additional financing couldn't be raised or shifting real estate markets and rising interest rates took a toll.

Often we are asked to get into limited partnerships for tax reasons. In these kinds of arrangements, income is calculated at the partnership level but can then be attributed to the individual participants, which translates into numerous tax advantages. But you must never lose sight of the fact that the investment must stand on its own two feet. Tax considerations are important, but they should never outweigh the basic merit of the deal. Again, I have seen dozens of investors lose all their money in a sour deal, only to face recapture by the tax authorities as well.

Limited partnerships can work well if all participants bring something to the table and the entire deal is aboveboard and unambiguous. For all others, it's buyer beware.

THE REAL ESTATE INVESTMENT TRUST (REIT)

A REIT is sort of like a mutual fund that invests solely in real estate projects. You put your money into a common pool, then properties are bought, sold, and moved around. The assumption is that the clever folks overseeing the REIT will make money from the moving hither and yon. And you, of course, will get rich as your share value appreciates.

The growth in popularity of REITs throughout North America since the mid-1990s has been astounding. The fast-rising stock market has seen huge pools of cash move into these income-producing vehicles. If you don't believe me, just look at the numbers. In 1991, these kinds of trusts owned 50,000 condo units in the United States. Just five years later, in 1996, REITs held a reported 600,000 units. That's a 1,200 percent increase!

Now, although the investment medium is the same, there is a big difference between investing in a real estate limited partnership and investing in a REIT. When you invest in a limited partnership, you are almost always locked in until the property is disposed of. If circumstances change for the worse, you're still in there for the duration. But a REIT is traded on the stock exchange, and thus you have liquidity.

REITs also usually have a specific mandate as to what they can do. If they invest in income-producing property, there are regulations governing how they distribute the dividends. Again, this is an element that you don't find in the average limited partnership.

REITs have not always been successful, but they do generally perform better than limited partnerships that contain provisions for investor redemption. The reason for this is that they don't have to sell the real estate to meet these redemptions. As a result, they can avoid selling if the market isn't right. Still, you must never lose sight of the fact that with all investments of this type, what you are really buying is the management team.

So should a REIT be your investment of choice? Well, first you must realize that, like most mutual funds that invest in real estate, REITs have had a chequered history. In the mid-1980s, for example, REITs in the United States and Canada experienced huge losses when business properties in certain cities got pounded. Some REITs saw solid gains in the period from 1993–97, but it's all relative. Most are again off in value today.

The most important thing is that you're aware of the essential difference between a REIT and a real estate mutual fund. Mutuals are open-ended, in that the client can ask to redeem the value of her shares at any time. This means that when markets cool slightly and investors want out, many funds find themselves carrying a heavy redemption load. And things snowball from there. Forced to sell into an already depressed market, the manager sees his fund lose even more value. This sends additional panicked investors rushing in with their unwanted paper, making things even worse. It's no fun for anyone.

REITs also rise and fall with real estate values, of course, but they are close-ended — that is, a predetermined number of units are issued and traded on the stock exchange. The value of the units is dependent upon the perceptions of stock-market investors. If the REIT is highly valued, it will be worth a lot of money. If it's not, it won't.

REITs also give the investor a piece of the assets held by the trust (proportionate to the amount invested, of course). Often, this means commercial properties. But this isn't as good as it may sound. The implied risks include the following:

- The buildings owned by the trust may not generate enough cash flow to carry them. This means a drop in income for the trustholders.
- If the stock market slips in general, REITs slide down too — even if an individual REIT has great assets.
- To get the maximum return for the minimum investment, REITs usually invest in highly leveraged properties. This means the risk is high.

The best advice I can give you if you really want to invest in a REIT is to research the trust carefully, paying particular attention to the past performance of the management team and/or the principals. (Many of today's REITs are yesterday's real estate mutual funds. Although they may look good on paper, they often have a history of pretty terrible performance.) Check out the actual properties (not the potential buys) owned by the fund, and don't be fooled by all the smoke and mirrors. We investigated a number of REITs in 1998 and concluded that they had paid too much for properties and would be underperforming in terms of expected income — and yet investors snapped them up. REITs are primarily a stock-market play, in other words, not a real estate one.

THE HOTEL-CONDO

We have come a long way since the original strata suites of the 1970s. Now we have two-level strata townhouses on top of a suite, suites on top of townhouses, a veritable hodgepodge of variations on the theme of residential home ownership with shared common areas. But hold it ... only residential? We also have strata warehouses, strata mini-storage, strata retail space, strata office space — again, all designed to provide living, working, and storage space for individual owners who share some common purpose of use.

But as earth-shaking as the strata title introduction was, we now have something just as revolutionary: the "hotel" strata unit (where each room is like a separate condominium). After sputtering about for some eighteen years (with some huge losses for early investors), strata hotel units finally seem to have hit their stride.

It all started at Whistler. When their performance was measured against that of the traditional categories of real estate, these new hotel-type units proved to be selling like the proverbial hotcakes. But what was all the excitement about? Statistics indicated that single-family homes and lots appreciated in value quickly, but the so-called phase I units (which carried an implied moral obligation to rent) appreciated more slowly. And the phase II units (which carried a legal obligation to rent, with only limited personal use) hardly rose in value at all. Yet people couldn't wait to jump in. And because of this success, a bewildering array of "differing use" options were added to the later phase II, culminating in the new hotel-condos. (For more detail on these units, see also chapter 21.)

Well — you may be saying — who can argue with blow-out success? I can, that's who. I have seen many people buy units based on a projected occupancy rate of 60 to 65 percent in markets that operate at between 35 and 55 percent. But more worrisome than the occupancy rates is the fact that not all hotels are alike. The payoff to investors lies in the management contract, and this differs from project to project. How much does the hotel cost to operate? What guarantees does the management company hold? Is it able to honour those guarantees? What performance bonuses will be paid? Are the projected net profits achievable? Who earns what first? If the hotel loses money, is the investor vulnerable to additional cash calls? As usual, it's crucial to have the answers to these and numerous other questions before you even think about buying.

Of course, the success at Whistler (where strata apartments sold for approximately $250 per foot and hotel units for up to $600 per foot) raised the eyebrows and stirred the lust of Vancouver developers. Not surprisingly, a blizzard of hotel-type deals hit Canadian markets starting in 1993, and new deals are still being introduced every day.

What Exactly Is a Hotel-Condo?

You've probably noticed that I often use the term "hotel-type deals." I do this because there are a lot of different horses in the stable, and distinguishing the thoroughbreds from the hacks is no easy feat. For the most part, however, these hotel-type units fall into one of the four following categories:

1. *The traditional condominium.* You own your four walls yourself and have common area joys and obligations with others. Inside the unit, you decorate to your delight. Cleaning is a privilege you keep to yourself.

2. *The furnished condominium.* These units are much like traditional condominiums, except that you get furniture as well (and pay for it).

3. *The furnished and serviced condominium.* These units, also often called executive suites, are bought by a purchaser who then has the option of placing his or her unit into a rental pool. Units are rented on a "minimum monthly stay" basis, and they come with maid service and, in some cases, room service.

4. *The flagship hotel operating with true daily bookings.* Several of these projects have come to market in the past year or so. As always, it's important that you do your research and ask questions to find out how these hotels really operate. To what extent is the chain affiliation applicable? Who really manages the property? And to what extent is the unit defined as a security (and hence possibly subject to severe restrictions on liquidity and resale)?

This whole investment arena became even more exciting when developers began to notice some highly successful sales of hotel-type units in major cities. Believe it or not, buildings that offered 600- to 900-square-foot units at approximately $250 per square foot (unfurnished) were sometimes left sitting, while nearby hotel-type units of 400 to 500 square feet at approximately $350 per square foot sold like there was no tomorrow.

The perception was that these buildings would operate like daily hotels but carry residential zoning (i.e., only monthly rentals allowed). Advertisements promised features that were not covered in the operating budget (in one case, ads promised concierge services and twenty-four-hour security, but neither was allowed for in the budget!), and boasted that investors would be enjoying a 50 percent rental return within five years.

Does it all sound too good to be true? Well, that's because it was. Yet many investors felt no need to be sceptical. Ignoring the statistics on vacancy rates, the tumultuous history of ventures like these, and the fact that the guarantees offered by the developers were insufficient and could not be verified, investors flocked to these deals like flies to honey. When you're hot, you're hot.

Of course not all hotel-type units are alike. Some were marketed without excessive promises or worthless guarantees. One notable developer even said, "We don't give a guarantee. There is no magic, no smoke and mirrors, at our hotel. If you believe in our flag, if you believe in Vancouver's growth, if you believe in the superb management contract we negotiated, we want you. A guarantee contract simply adds cost." Almost refreshing to hear, isn't it?

The point is that if you're interested in buying a hotel, make sure you are, in fact, buying a hotel and not an apartment that looks like a hotel. But even if you buy a so-called flag hotel, you must understand that you are in the hotel business, with all that implies. Flags are often bought for their reservation systems and stature but then operated by someone else. If this is your situation, you'd better study that operating agreement with a magnifying glass. These kinds of units are sold by extolling the benefits, glossing over drawbacks, and stressing the association with the company whose name is behind the hotel. People get the idea that they are investing in Hyatt or Hilton or Marriott, but if you examine the fine print you find that this simply isn't the case. These large chains will lease their name and allow access to their reservation system, but otherwise they have nothing to do with the hotel's operation.

In the end, investors have to appreciate that a serviced apartment with a "guaranteed" revenue will be successful only if the project has the ability to generate the returns forecast and the financial strength to support the guarantee. If a two-year-old suite in your average metropolitan centre is selling for between $200 and $300 per square foot, you should think long and hard before you pay $450 to $600 per foot for a hotel unit. And don't forget that you should always be thinking about resale potential. In the words of one major marketer, "Until we are sure that there is a secondary market [someone to sell the original units to], we will not be in the strata hotel business." Very wise indeed.

If You Still Want to Buy . . .

1. Understand what you are buying: a straight apartment unit, a furnished one, a serviced and furnished one, a monthly rental hotel, or a fully operating hotel.
2. Understand that if there is a guarantee with a mandated rental pool, you are buying a security and not traditional real estate.
3. Understand that if you are buying a security, you could have a problem with the resale. In fact, there is no proven secondary market for these units.
4. Understand the management contract that the hotel negotiates with the operating company. Ask yourself these questions:
   a) Who is the actual operator of the hotel? (The flag may have nothing to do with day-to-day operations.)
   b) What is the operator's experience?
   c) How much of the performance is guaranteed?

d) What is the fixed annual fee, and will that fee be paid regardless of the operator's performance and the hotel's bottom line?

e) Does the promoter of the project understand the hotel business? Has he negotiated a great management deal on behalf of his investors?

5. Is the performance guarantee secured by a realistic amount of money, and is that money accessible if it is needed?

6. Are you liable for your mortgage only? If the hotel is operating in the red, will you be expected to step up to the plate for a cash call?

7. Are you responsible for the performance of the restaurant, the parking lots, the banquet facilities, and the commercial lease space? (No, this is not an added benefit for you — it is a way for the hotel to insure income for itself.)

THE LAST WORD

Let me finish up by saying that the average person just doesn't have the financial, business, and real estate experience (not to mention the time) to do an adequate analysis of these kinds of investments. There are too many ways to lose and only a couple of ways to win. I believe it makes much more sense for the average investor to put money in conventional real estate. But if you're *still* tempted, make sure you ask the right questions and let common sense be your guide.

In Essence

◇ Whenever you are a minority participant in a venture, you are in effect handing your money to someone and saying, "Here you are. Take this money and do the best you can with it."

◇ Most scams are found in the area of limited partnerships. Because investors believe their potential losses are limited, they are sometimes less rigorous than they should be about examining a deal.

> Any investment must stand on its own two feet. Tax considerations are important, but they should never outweigh the basic merit of the deal.

◇ With REITs and all similar investments, what you are really buying is the management team.

◇ If you're interested in buying a hotel, make sure you are, in fact, buying a hotel and not an apartment that looks like a hotel.

18

Construction
and Development

In development, one mistake can land you in
bankruptcy court.

If you have a burning desire to have a career in construction and development, by all means go out and learn how to do it. But be forewarned: no other area of business has a higher casualty rate. And since one of the central points of this entire book is that the returns for real estate investors should be commensurate with the risks, I would advise you to think twice before setting off down this road. Whenever the returns are not commensurate with the risks, the situation should, in my opinion, be avoided.

Historically and statistically, the field of construction and development is a bad bet. For one thing, the learning curve is very long and very steep. Until you learn what you need to know, you're going to be play-ing someone else's game — and we all know what that means. But if part of your investment objective is to have that same rush of adrenaline that you get when riding a roller coaster, then construction and development should be ideal for you.

Before we go any further, let's clarify things by defining our terms. What do we mean by construction and development? Well, before I explain what it is, let's first talk a bit about what it is not. When you buy a lot and build a single house on it, you are engaged in construction and development, to be sure. But that's not what we're talking about here. Building a single home or even a duplex is nothing compared with building a multi-home subdivision or a multi-unit apartment or condo project. If you build a single home and it doesn't appeal to any buyers, you can move into it yourself, give it to the bank, or lower the price until someone purchases it. You may be financially bent but you won't be broken. The damage is contained. With a multi-unit project, how-ever, you are going to be in some serious hot water if you miss the target. And the difference between joy and misery may be only a few months. Because many larger projects operate on margins of 15 percent annual profits, it doesn't take too long a period of no sales to wipe out profits. And the carrying costs go on, even if sales do not.

Even so, this is a seductive area of activity. Newspapers are constantly running items about mega-projects that sold out in a matter of days. And human nature being what it is, we all want a piece of the action. But those same newspapers also often carry accounts of projects that have been on the market for years and are still not sold out. What makes the difference?

The difference is the developer. The successful developer is a better judge of what to build where and at what price. He has that immeasurable, unquantifiable element called talent. He can put himself into the psyche of the consumer and know instinctively what will work and what will not. I'm telling you right now that if you don't have the talent, don't even sail away from the dock.

Of course, even talented and experienced developers have failures — and it's usually a question of timing. As one developer friend told me, "I have an engineering degree and a degree in architecture. I can put up a very fine building with good amenities and lose my shirt simply because I come to the market at the wrong time. Yet I have seen shoddy buildings . . . sell in a weekend because the marketplace perceived that it was a great time to buy and the developer spent a fortune to create a pre-selling circus. It is a frustrating business." Indeed.

So here comes the important lesson: The average investor doesn't really care why a project succeeds or fails. He needs only to consider if the return is commensurate with the risks and if the investment fits his overall objectives. Everything else is just commentary.

In the case of the multi-unit development, the damage can be extensive indeed if sales projections aren't met. And once a loss has been suffered, everyone wants to know what caused it. But the smarter course is to focus on successful projects and determine what it took those developers to get to that point.

THE LAST WORD

It takes about the same amount of education and experience to become a successful developer as it does to become any other kind of professional. The big difference is that other professionals can learn from their mistakes and pass that new-found knowledge onto their clients. When a developer makes a mistake, he winds up in bankruptcy court.

"All right," you say. "What I'll do is find a developer who knows what it's all about and I'll partner up with him." At that point, you cease to be a developer yourself and you start to be a mooch. This is never a good idea. You'll wind up as either a lender with no security or a buyer of securities who's the last guy on the list to be paid. Trust me, there are much better things you could be doing with your money.

In Essence

> No other business has as high a casualty rate as construction and development.

> In this field, the difference between joy and misery may be only a few months. It doesn't take much of a downturn to wipe out profits.

> The developer is often the only difference between a successful project and failed one.

> The investor should ask himself if the return is commensurate with the risks and if the investment fits his overall objectives.

19

Selecting Your Experts and Advisers

Experto credite. [Trust one who has gone through it.]
— *Virgil*, Aeneid

Experts have specific knowledge and can show you which hoops to jump through and how to do so most effectively. Advisers have had life experiences that make their opinions valuable and their advice worth taking. The problem is that most people confuse the two functions and use an expert for advice or an adviser for expertise. This usually ends in inconvenience at best, disaster at worst.

Another common mistake people make is to assume that the person who has expertise in one field also has expertise in a related field. Experts are business people who charge by the hour, so they're not likely to turn you away even if they know in their heart of hearts that they are not the best ones for the job. They are often not averse to a little on-the-job training — especially when it's at your expense.

This is what makes this area so dangerous and also so important. We go to experts to get access to the special knowledge that they have and we don't. But as laypeople, we are not in a position to make value judgements about their suitability for the job. The real estate investment business is especially complex, of course, and so the task of choosing the right expert is that much more difficult. That's why you're better off using an adviser to help you select an expert than you are selecting one all on your own.

A CAUTIONARY TALE

To illustrate the dangers inherent in choosing the wrong expert, let me tell you about a case that has been in the newspapers lately. The case involves investors who bought into a co-op housing project thinking it was a condominium. Now, first you need to understand that in a condominium, you own your own unit individually and everyone owns the common areas in concert. In a co-op, by contrast, the co-op itself owns the units and everything else and investors own shares of the co-op. This difference becomes highly significant when someone defaults. If you stop making payments on your condo, the mortgage holder will foreclose and that's the end of that. But when one person defaults on his mortgage in a co-op, the other members are all responsible for it.

In this particular instance, the building had some construction deficiencies and the place leaked like a sieve. Because the cost of repairs was almost more than what they owed on their mortgages, some of the people who had bought in with very small down payments just walked away. They decided to cut their losses, in other words. This left high and dry those who had made sizeable down payments and those who had paid cash. They had too much already invested to cut and run, but the burden for repairs and defaulted mortgages was growing heavier with each passing day.

Yes, yes, that's all terrible, you're probably saying. But what has any of this got to do with choosing the wrong experts and advisers? Well, two things. First, the developers of the co-op made a poor choice when they selected the lawyer who did the paperwork for them. His job was to make sure that they were colouring within the lines, as we used to say in kindergarten, and he failed miserably. Second, the people who bought units in the co-op either made an unwise decision not to seek advice or were poorly counselled by the so-called experts they did retain.

Because the entire deal was filled with undotted i's and uncrossed t's, all kinds of people got caught in the trap. The developers of the project wanted to blame their lawyer because he didn't provide them with the safeguards they so desperately needed. Of course, these safeguards — by which I mean a brutally frank explanation of what could happen if things went wrong — would have made the units difficult to sell. Being candid with a prospective purchaser about the downside of a deal is like putting another obstacle in her path, and thus will have a negative impact on sales. For his part, the lawyer wanted to blame the developers because, instead of alerting their customers to all the potential dangers, they chose to gloss over some of the stickier aspects of the deal.

Everyone who bought a unit had ample opportunity to seek expert advice before putting pen to paper. In fact, if they'd done that, some might not have bought at all, and thus would not have ended up in the untenable position they did. Of course, some of those who bought probably did seek advice first. These unfortunate people likely just went to the wrong source, and the end result was the same.

If you don't want to make these kinds of mistakes, you need to learn how to pick the right expert and the right adviser for the job. Don't count on these people to tell you themselves when they are venturing into uncharted waters. In my experience, people will seldom admit that they don't really know what they are doing.

At the same time, you must be aware that your professionals — that is, your lawyers, accountants, real estate agents, etc. — are there to *save* you money, not *make* you money. Lawyers are for dotting i's and crossing t's so that you stay out of jail and keep your property. Accountants are for keeping track of your money and ensuring that you pay as little of it to the government as possible. Real estate agents facilitate the deals that you find for yourself or those that they find for you but you decide to pursue. That's it! Not one of these professionals is there to make you money. That's your job.

GET UNBIASED AND INDEPENDENT ADVICE

When it comes to advice (as opposed to expertise), you must find someone who has been down the road you want to travel and motivate that person to give you his advice. Let me rephrase that — you have to motivate that person to *sell* you his advice.

This is usually not an impossible task. For example, I consider myself knowledgeable in the area of real estate investment, and my advice is for sale through newsletters, faxes, tapes, and lectures. In fact, most advisers out there will sell you advice. The problem is finding the right source. When you're evaluating potential advisers, there are several key questions you should put to yourself. Is the advice unbiased and independent? Is the adviser selling anything else? Will he or she benefit personally by steering me in this or that direction? Questions like these will help you choose the right person for the job.

Your adviser is like the navigator of a ship (you, of course, are the captain!). He is going to set your course, directing you towards this expert or that one and steering you well clear of any hazards. This is why it's so important to choose an adviser who is experienced, competent, and well-intentioned. You want to be sure that he doesn't send you off course by recommending the wrong expert for your specific situation.

For the simple stuff, a good real estate lawyer is all you will need. If you start getting fancy, however, and put together a deal that involves a group of people, you're going to need a securities lawyer. If you begin to make some decent money, you may find that you need a tax lawyer. If, on the other hand, you get into financial trouble or become involved with other people who are in financial trouble, you may find yourself in need of a bankruptcy lawyer. And it goes on from there.

In each of these situations, you want someone who already knows his specialty. Many times, you'll find that your ability to survive trouble is in direct relation to the quality of your lawyer and his suitability for the task at hand. Of course, no top professional in any area would take on a task for which he didn't have the expertise (that's what referrals are for), but in this imperfect world we sometimes find that there are more horses' rear ends than there are horses.

We've all heard the old saying that a man who acts as his own lawyer has a fool for a client. Most of us subscribe to this point of view, and so we leave the legal manoeuvrings to those who know what they're doing. But when it comes to accounting, we seem pretty willing to dabble at it ourselves. And most of the time this is all right — except when we get to the area of income tax.

I suppose what we should really do is separate in our minds the concepts of bookkeeping and tax planning. Most people have no trouble with bookkeeping, which is more about maintaining careful records than anything else, but tax planning tends to get complicated. It is very important that you understand all the tax ramifications of your investments, and that you claim all the deductions and credits you have coming to you. Sometimes things you miss out on are gone forever, remember, and any mistakes will cost you money. This is why a good accountant can be indispensable.

Like lawyers and accountants, real estate agents can save you a lot of money if you handle them right. Although some people don't view them as on a par with the first two, I can tell you from considerable experience that the good agents are every bit as professional as their colleagues in the legal and accounting fields.

I like a realtor who doesn't argue with me when I want to write a low offer. I am also the proverbial tire-kicker, though I do eventually always buy. One realtor whose grey hair is probably entirely due to me has shown me properties beyond the proverbial line of duty, but he also sold me seven homes over a ten-year period. In other words, I'll stick with a realtor who is prepared to stick with me. Commissions don't worry me. I want a professional, and if I find one I gladly pay a professional's fee. My main concern is simply that he gets the job done.

Although it is possible to build relationships that continue over the years — and I have done this in a dozen different areas — most of your involvement with real estate agents will be on a piecemeal basis. You want to find someone who has achieved a delicate balance: he's busy enough to be successful, but he's not so successful that he's too busy to give you the attention you require.

My point through this whole section is that there is no need to go out and reinvent the wheel. Your sole task should be to select the professional you want to use. Most of the time, you can narrow the field by asking someone you trust for a referral. Approach another real estate investor (a successful one), for example, and ask him to recommend someone who can do the job you need done. If you don't know of anyone to ask in your own field, you can ask a person in a related field. A good tax lawyer will usually know who the good securities lawyers are, for instance.

But remember that you can't get any answer at all if you don't ask the question. This is what allows you to build cumulatively on the experience and expertise of those who have walked the road before you.

THE LAST WORD

Up to this point, we have talked only about the necessity of having these experts and advisers, and about how to select them. For most people, that's the entire process. The common attitude is that once you select a professional, all your decision making ends. From that point forward, these people tell you what to do and how to do it, and at the end of the month they send you a bill and you pay it.

If you live in a city where there's only one lawyer who specializes in the area you need, that probably would be the end of it. But the more common reality is that the Yellow Pages are filled with the names of all sorts of people who can play the role you need. It's important for you to know this, to be sure, but it's even more important for the professional you're considering to know that you know it.

Let's say it's your first meeting with a prospective lawyer. After you have outlined what you want him to do, you should ask him to describe his fee structure in plain language. You want to know how much he charges, how the charges are calculated, and what kind of reporting you can expect. The answers he gives are nowhere near as important as the mere fact that you've asked the questions. He now knows that you're watching, and this alone is going to save you money.

Let me illustrate this with a brief story about an optometrist who was teaching his son the business. After he had taught the boy everything he needed to know about optometry, the father sat down with his son and said, "I am now going to teach you how to charge for your goods and services. When you are sitting in front of a patient, fitting the glasses, you say to him, 'The glasses are one hundred dollars.' Watch his face very carefully. If he doesn't flinch, you say, 'That's for the frames. The lenses are another hundred dollars.' You continue to watch his face. And if he doesn't flinch, you say, 'Each!'"

What's the lesson from this? No matter what a professional quotes as his fee structure or hourly rate, you have to flinch. If he sees you flinching, he just may keep some kind of rein on his charges. Remember that anything you pay him will be deducted from your net profits.

Once you have had this initial discussion, you may think you have the money question settled. But you have to keep monitoring the situation. It is important for you to be clear on what you want your professionals to accomplish for you so that you will know if the benchmarks are being met. If they are not, you must find out who's responsible. If the problem's originating on your side of the fence, it has to be fixed immediately. If it's originating on his side of the fence, it has to be fixed much sooner than that.

The single biggest mistake people make in dealing with professionals is believing they practise some arcane craft that is a mystery to us lesser mortals. Treat these people exactly as you would anyone else you hire to do work for you. The sooner you demystify them, the better your relationship will be.

This is another reason why I am such a big advocate of the written plan. When you have your plan in writing, you have concrete benchmarks by which to measure progress. If your mileposts are not being met, you will know that either your expectations are unrealistic or someone isn't doing his job. If that someone is you, you have to change your own behaviour or lower your expectations. But if that someone is one of your professionals, you have to demand changes in his performance. Again, if you're watching and measuring all the time, you'll know when to reward good performance and penalize bad.

Now we come to a sticky subject. Every once in a while it becomes necessary to fire a professional. This is rarely easy and it's never pleasant. Remember that the kindest way to cut off a dog's tail is not one inch at a time. Be forthright and frank. Sit down with your professional, state your complaint, and tell him you're making other arrangements. But be prepared to pay his bill (assuming that's not what the disagreement is about) if you want your records delivered to you. Also, you should try to have new arrangements lined up before you terminate your old ones.

The most important thing to remember about your professionals is that they will make the difference between average results and excellent results. If you select and manage them wisely and use them effectively, you can get optimum returns. But it's a three-step process. You have to know what questions to ask, you have to actually ask the questions once you know them, and then you have to act on the advice you get.

In Essence

◇ You're always better off using an adviser to help you select an expert than you are selecting one all on your own.

> Don't count on your professionals to tell you when they are venturing into uncharted waters. People will seldom admit that they don't really know what they're doing.
> Be aware that your professionals are there to *save* you money, not *make* you money. That's your job.
> There is no need to reinvent the wheel. Try to build on the experience and expertise of those who have walked the road before you.
> You must be clear on what you want your professionals to accomplish for you. That way, you will know if your benchmarks are (or are not) being met.

20

Technology: Enemy or Friend to Real Estate?

For I dipp'd into the future, far as human eye could see,
Saw the Vision of the world, and all the wonder that
would be.

— *ALFRED, LORD TENNYSON,* "LOCKSLEY HALL"

Not a minute goes by without our being peppered with information about the New Age, the Internet, e-mail, and the shift to a global community. Today, talk of technology permeates everything.

Ours is a future that will be dominated by information that is ready, accessible, and interactive. Indeed, it can easily be argued that the free flow of this type of information has already changed the world, quietly raising the Iron Curtain and toppling communism. Whether we like it or not, society is constantly fragmenting and reforming.

And all of this, of course, has had an impact on our everyday lives. The information explosion has driven down prices, raised quality, and killed off non-aligned competitors by the thousands. The well-informed new consumer can compare and contrast before buying — and not only across town, but also across the globe. Gone are the days when people were loyal to only one supplier, retailer, government, or even ideology. This is a mix-and-match world, and we can embrace and discard as suits our purposes.

Fair enough, you may say. But what does all this have to do with real estate? Well, I predict that the next five years will see a huge shift in how real estate is being appraised, assessed, marketed, sold, distributed, and registered. And this will all be because of readily available information, demanding and able consumers, and ever-faster and more affordable computers. The same revolution that drove down the cost of a stock transaction to fractions of a cent is now shaking up the real estate industry from top to bottom.

WHOEVER CONTROLS THE INFORMATION CONTROLS THE GAME

When Henry and Arthur Block, the founding fathers of Vancouver's real estate business, ran Block Bros. in the 1970s, they owned the market. For several years in a row, Block Bros. outperformed its ten biggest competitors combined. It was a giant looming above the vertically challenged.

What made Block Bros. so good? Did it have better salespeople? A better vision? To a point, yes. But its biggest weapon was information. The company had built up a comprehensive catalogue full of jealously guarded information that was accessible only to its own people. Throughout the 1970s, Block Bros. refused to list its properties on the multiple listing service (MLS) of the real estate board. When it did co-operate with the competition, it did so only on its own terms.

And then along came the year 1980. The real estate boards and the competition created their own MLS catalogues. At the same time, fortress Block Bros. caved in to the continued pressure from within, and decided to allow its own salespeople to pick up some extra commissions by using MLS as well. The wall was breached.

But what neither Block Bros. nor any of its competitors realized was that by shifting information — that is, real inventory — to the real estate boards' MLS, they were actually handing over their true power — control of that information — to the boards as well. Because the individual salesperson could, in effect, own the information through her board's MLS, she became more and more independent. Real estate companies did try to adapt and accommodate the ever-increasing demands of their sales forces, but alas, the big weapon, exclusive access to information, was no longer owned by them.

Until the early 1990s, the slugfest raged on. Big real estate firms were collapsing everywhere, bled dry by salespeople who played their "employers" off against each other. These salespeople — armed with as much information as they could possibly need, demanding and getting all of the commission, loyal only to themselves — controlled the field.

Of course, I am making no value judgements here. Events unfolded as they had to, given the unstoppable flow of information and the evolution of the well-prepared, fickle, well-educated salesperson. My point is simply that the same pressures that put the key information into the hands of that salesperson are now putting it into the hands of the consumer via the Internet.

This consumer-driven virtual marketplace has no room (or need) for the middleman. Dell Computers sells $10 million worth of product a day from its Web site, and the company fully expects to earn 50 percent of its revenue from the Net by 2001. Amazon.com sells 60,000 books per day through its site, and even smaller players like yours truly can sell many thousand dollars worth of merchandise to customers in places that would have been utterly inaccessible in the past. Who needs a go-between?

Information has always meant power. But where it was once used to separate the few from the many, it is today the great leveller, a true example of democracy in action. Small wonder that the real estate industry, like most every other industry, is experiencing a shift of such monumental proportions.

So is this a case of the salespeople getting a taste of their own medicine? Will they be shut out in the cold by the consumer just as they themselves did to the large agencies in the 1980s? Not necessarily. There is some breathing room, a window during which smart real estate firms and agents can adjust, shift, and learn to benefit from the coming changes. Many real estate boards are sniffing the wind and leaping aboard the Internet bandwagon in a mad bid just to be there.

Mega sites like www.realtor.com in the United States and www.mls.ca in Canada are representing organized real estate, but there are hundreds of other players, each with several hundred thousand listings. Microsoft's entry (www.homeadvisor.com) is a huge resource site, and even Joe Public can place his properties there directly. Smaller players have seen a huge increase in traffic in the past few years; my own www.jurock.com site went from 10,000 hits per month in 1995 to more than 3 million hits per month in early 1999. As more and more customers get used to buying on the Net, this trend will increase.

Many big companies are using technology to boot out the middleman. For example, CMHC's EMILY computer program, with its four-level market evaluation (local area stats, provincial stats, economic outlook, and lender criteria), was reported to have eliminated 95 percent of all residential appraisals for CMHC-insured properties by the middle of 1999. Talk about putting pressure on the appraisal industry. But don't despair. The sky hasn't fallen yet, and there's still time to prepare your ground.

The World Wide Web remains a bewildering place to visit. Millions of people are still getting lost, and numerous sites have either too little information or too much information that is worthless. But any mine requires a lot of surface work first. Within the next five years, the Internet will transform itself into a cohesive, consumer-driven information system.

In the meantime, a tremendous sea change has already swept the real estate industry. Since 1986, some 21,000 offices in the United States have shut down; in Canada, another 2,400 have fallen by the wayside. The realtor population in the U.S. dropped from 1,050,000 in 1989 to 640,000 in 1999. In Canada, the ranks are down by about 30,000 in that same period.

What does the future hold? We'll probably see a smaller number of independent salespeople doing more deals for less commission. Also, the commission payment may shift more to the selling side from the listing side. Investors will have easier, faster access to deals. And everything will become more performance-based, with fickle consumers demanding more service for less money.

FOURTEEN TRENDS TO WATCH FOR

When it comes to the Internet's potential to revolutionize society, we have barely seen the tip of the iceberg. But even this small glimpse suggests the many rewards available to individuals and companies that are willing and able to take advantage of these new opportunities.

The changes that lie ahead may be frightening, but they are also full of promise. What follows is a list of a few of the changes I believe are coming (and some of which are already here).

1. *The power of the consumer.* The real estate industry, in particular, is in the throes of a major transformation. The power has shifted from companies and agents to individual consumers. I believe that the whole buying-and-selling process will originate with people's home computers in the future.

2. *Information at your fingertips.* Today's consumer wants to be educated and well-informed. To meet this need, companies will move to provide on-line access to extensive, detailed information, free of charge. Consumers will be able to school themselves in everything from the

basics to advanced negotiating skills and how to perform sophisticated market evaluations.

3. *Neighbourhood information.* Thanks to the Internet, you will be able
to order crime statistics by neighbourhood, school-match reports
(to find a school that meets your family's criteria), school statistics
(to find out where they're located, what levels are taught, whether
they're public or private, etc.), and trend information (such as
population growth, job growth, and so on).

4. *Legal information.* Sites will provide easy-to-understand explanations
of the legal differences of types of ownership (e.g., strata condo,
single-family, mixed-use, etc.); detailed explanations and evaluations;
comparisons of the differences by actual building; and so on.

5. *Demographic-mix reports.* This kind of report includes information
on a neighbourhood's racial composition, age and income distribution, religious climate, etc. There are some huge implications here!

6. *Mortgage information.* You'll be able to compare the best rates (as
opposed to the stated rates) of *all* financial institutions nationwide.
Sites will include detailed information on the exact products
offered.

7. *Mortgages from home.* After rates are compared, you can apply for
approvals from your own home and get an answer in a few minutes.

8. *On-line mortgage calculators.* These tools will allow you to adjust
length of term, size of payments, and a thousand other options until
you come up with a scenario that fits your personal circumstances.

9. *Legal conveyancing rates.* These you'll be able to compare by individual quote and law firm.

10. *Appraisal rates.* You'll be able to compare these by appraisal group, individual quote, and appraisal firm.

11. *Home searches.* A buyer will be able to search for available homes by his family's personal criteria (city, neighbourhood, property type, etc.).

12. *Market comparables.* Sellers will be able to perform full comparable searches of recent and similar listings. Independent on-line market evaluations will also be available.

13. *Pushed information.* Buyers *and* sellers can list their wants and needs (e.g., three-bedroom home, no more than $100,000, family neigh-bourhood), then receive e-mails on available properties fitting the criteria until the right one is found.

14. *Credit reports.* Get a credit report on yourself before you do any-thing else.

WHAT ELSE IS COMING?

The advancements I've outlined above will contribute to the trans-formation of the real estate industry, but the transformation in technology will be equally as important. As Internet download speeds increase, we will be able to access 360-degree virtual reality images. Homeowners and real estate agents will be able to upload pictures of listed properties, which interested buyers can then view in as much detail as they would like. And by 2001, we'll have real-time on-line video. Buyers will be able to view a one- to five-minute clip of any avail-able property easily in the privacy of their own homes. These factors, in combination, will pave the way for the changes I've listed below, and many more besides.

1. *Map-based systems will drive the New World.* Some systems already allow map-based detailed viewing of properties. In the future, this will explode. Angle views, multiple pictures, and hard information (including selling histories) will all be available at the push of a button. You'll be able to put your cursor on the corner of an image of a home, and the computer will calculate the square footage. Shadows can be used to determine the height of a property within three centimetres.

2. *The assessment authorities will go into competition with real estate boards.* When it comes to providing sales information to the public in a careful, predetermined way, the assessment authorities will give real estate boards a run for their money. In fact, these authorities already have more information on houses than you can begin to imagine. The pressure to earn extra income will drive them to market.

3. *MLS turf wars will increase.* The turf war for MLS listings throughout the United States and Canada will heat up. Already there has been at least one lawsuit. In 1998, a New Jersey superior court judge temporarily ended a turf war between MLS boards when he ordered Garden State MLS to continue to share listings with New Jersey MLS until another hearing could be held. (Garden State MLS — which is owned by Weichert Realtors, Coldwell Banker, Prudential, and Burgdorff/ERA — had instructed brokers to stop placing their listings in the rival NJMLS, which is jointly operated by two Bergen County boards.) Microsoft, meanwhile, is accusing realtor.com of offering special deals to its participating companies; at the same time, Microsoft itself makes deals with brokers for *free* lifetime listings.

4. *Mega players will blur the distinction about who can distribute real estate information.* In late 1998, more than 500 Re/Max brokers in forty states signed agreements to place their listings on the Microsoft HomeAdvisor site, just weeks after Re/Max's international head-

quarters in Denver announced it was embracing HomeAdvisor's chief rival, realtor.com, as its Web service vendor. Clearly, the battle between major Internet players like Microsoft and the realtor-only sites will intensify.

5. *Affinity programs will flourish, cutting into commissions.* AmeriNet Financial Systems reported that it did $50 million in business in one month in 1999, the strongest month in the history of the loan brokerage. It credited the results to wide general acceptance of its Consumer Advantage Real Estate Services (CARES) program, which offers customers rebates on real estate commissions. The CARES program is currently active in Washington, Oregon, California, Colorado, Arizona, Maryland, Virginia, and the District of Columbia. Programs like these will soon be widespread.

WHAT LIES AHEAD

According to an ActivMedia study, real estate is the industry most likely to lead explosive e-commerce revenue growth over the next few years. And while MLS turf wars and competition between mega-players will increase, I believe none of that will ultimately matter. The relentless onslaught of the information-rich consumer will continue to cut into commissions, dramatically change the nature of services provided, and overwhelm companies that are caught between the old world and the new. Even the organizers of a recent real estate conference in the U.S. seemed to realize this, remarking, "The day is rapidly coming when e-commerce and the real estate transaction will be a seamless experience — an automated real estate process that is friction free and liberated from unnecessary fees." I can only assume that these "unnecessary fees" include appraisal fees, legal fees, placement fees, mortgage fees, and commissions.

Meanwhile, four powerful forces will alter the telecommunications landscape and revolutionize how we acquire, transform, and communicate information. These forces are regulatory reform, cross-border alliances, emerging infrastructure, and technological advances. But all these changes mean opportunity if you can originate information that no one else has or interpret information in a way no one else has thought of. Countless new jobs will emerge for HTML programmers; intranet writers; individuals who can create map-based systems; virtual reality photographers; and consultants, interpreters, and specialized marketing professionals.

The consumer of real estate, once he's learned the most expeditious ways to find and retrieve the information he needs, will have a much simpler world. The transaction process will increasingly be streamlined. From the privacy of his own home, a buyer will be able to specify what kind of home he wants, how much he wants to pay, what kind of neighbourhood he prefers, even the level of income he wants his new neighbours to have. After posting his needs, he will be able to review at his leisure the daily e-mails that will be sent to him automatically from a variety of competing companies. He will download 360-degree images of the listings he likes and only then look for a negotiator. Since he will have been pre-approved for a mortgage at the very best rate possible, the negotiations will be quick and painless. The whole process will take only a fraction of the time of a traditional real estate transaction.

This is a world that was made for the sophisticated, well-informed consumer of the new millennium. Whether you like it or not, a new day has dawned and this world is already here.

◇

In Essence

◇ Gone are the days when people were loyal to only one supplier, retailer, government, or even ideology. This is a mix-and-match world.

⟩ The next five years will see a huge shift in how real estate is being appraised, assessed, marketed, sold, distributed, and registered.

> The same pressures that once put key information into the hands of the real estate salesperson are now putting it into the hands of the consumer.

◇ The consumer-driven marketplace has no room for the middleman.

◇ Real estate is the industry most likely to lead explosive e-commerce revenue growth over the next few years.

21

Buying
Out of Town

God made the country, and man made the town.
— WILLIAM COWPER, THE TASK

People throughout North America are on the move. Californians move to Oregon and Arizona; New Yorkers joke at the rain but move to Washington. In Ontario, it was always the cottage on the lake. In B.C., it's the cabin in the mountains. Small towns, ski resorts, and resort areas have long teemed with former city slickers clutching cash and the hope for that elusive better quality of life. What is new is that now families actually uproot and move, bringing their jobs with them. Some commute back to the city, some live in both places, but most generate their know-how into a new enterprise.

Canada's population growth rate from the years 1991 to 1996

averaged 1.21 percent per year. In small towns and resort communities across Canada, however, the growth rate was twenty to thirty times that figure. Many went, saw, and bought. Most simply fell in love with the rolling hills, and the mountains. Some older yuppies bought without considering factors such as pace of life and local culture, isolation, lack of transportation, shortage of hospitals, and so on. And some came back, reality having destroyed the dream.

As I've tried to stress throughout this book, when investing in real estate, you must start by investing time in yourself. When you're considering buying out-of-town property, it becomes particularly important that you ask yourself the questions that will help you determine your investment objectives. What type of person are you? You dream of roughing it, but could you really? Are you a fixer-upper, or do you just think you are?

It's just as important, if not more so, to do your due diligence when considering an out-of-town property. The people you'll be dealing with will be strangers, so you have to be even more careful than you normally would. Also, be aware that every time you go into a new area, you are competing with people who live there and have the advantage of local knowledge. Sometimes that works against you and sometimes it works in your favour. (I can't explain why, but sometimes there are investment treasures right under the noses of the locals and they just don't see them. Someone can come in from out of town and snap up something really valuable. But you must *always* ask yourself why you're so lucky. Maybe the locals know something you don't.)

Finally, be sure to select the land that is right for your pocketbook, investment goals, and timeline. Every piece of recreational land has a use — that swamp might be just the thing for moneyed duck hunters, or perhaps that wind-buffeted cliff is the perfect spot for a hang-gliding enthusiast with a death wish — but that doesn't mean that every piece is the right piece for you. Whenever possible, think quality. According to those in the know, the right setting is often more important than the price per acre. A small but lovely piece on a knoll or next to a fishy creek will be often worth more than that really big chunk of nothing.

WHO BUYS OUT OF TOWN?

Understanding what kind of buyer you are will help you clarify your investment objectives. In my experience, most people who buy out-of-town properties match one of the six following personality types.

1. The Recreational Land Buyer
2. The Major Resort Buyer
3. The Profit-Seeking Buyer of Vacant Land
4. The Stressed-Out Seeker of Escape
5. The Offshore Escapee
6. The Opportunist

Let's examine each one of these individuals in a little more detail.

The Recreational Land Buyer

The recreational land buyer buys property for many reasons, and usually investment is way down the list. Sure, he'll take the money if he sells at a profit, but that isn't his primary purpose for buying.

This guy is an owner-user. He wants to boat, water-ski, hunt, fish, or just sit on the property and contemplate his navel. He wants privacy, control, and pride of ownership, in other words, and these things come only when you own that property yourself.

As a general rule, there is an inverse ratio between time and distance from an urban area and the value of the property — that is, as travel time from the urban area increases, the price of the property decreases. But this buyer generally wants to get to his property fast. Two to four hours of travel time is what he is looking for.

Of course, even if your main interest is personal use, you still want to keep half an eye on the investment aspect of your property. Before you buy, take into consideration amenities nearby such as rivers, lakes, ski hills, golf courses, and all the other features people look for when they are spending their recreation dollar.

The Major Resort Buyer

It is winter. You just came back from a day on the slopes, you have that warm glow of the second bottle of wine, and you say to yourself, "I should really buy here and kill two birds with one stone. I will have income *and* personal use." As I've said before, on the scale of financial mistakes, this one must be near the very top.

Anytime you confuse your investment objectives, I can guarantee that you'll be making some kind of mistake. In my experience, people are rarely able to combine the two objectives of personal use and investment in a single property. One reason is that the times you want to go skiing are the times everybody else does as well. Taking those times for yourself means a lot of lost revenue.

But more important, buying property at a resort is not like buying regular real estate. Resorts have real issues surrounding quality of construction, location, and investment class. You must understand what the implications of all these issues are before you buy. For example, if your resort consists only of a parking lot and a ski lift, the potential for capital appreciation is minimal. If you buy without any consideration of appreciation, you are really a recreation-only buyer.

If you plan to buy in a major resort, with all its quad chairs and restaurants and stores aplenty, you must be aware that many have restrictive covenants in place. The resort association knows that most people buy for holiday use only. Since visits rise tenfold in the winter, they restrict the personal use of units in a variety of ways. But you likely don't want to have your use restricted. And, like adding salt to the wound, these covenants usually translate into higher taxes and lower capital appreciation.

Let's take a minute to look at the different kinds of resort properties in a little more detail.

a) Single-family homes and building lots. This has been and will continue to be the best possible investment class in terms of price appreciation, primarily because use is unrestricted. I have seen well-located building lots rise in value by 400 percent over a two-year period, something that's unheard of in the other classes. Try to buy the best lot you can afford.

b) Single-family condos with a phase I covenant. This covenant implies a "moral obligation" to rent out your unit, but you can use it yourself at any time. These properties are really like regular strata units in town. Other than single-family homes, these are the only resort properties that I believe are safe in a market downturn. And of course, you can always mitigate your loss by moving in yourself or taking a lower rent.

c) Single-family condos with a phase II covenant. With these units, personal use is restricted to approximately fifty-six days a year and you are usually part of a management pool. You must pre-book your own use, and in some cases you'll even have to pay for the time. Any revenue collected from your unit belongs to everybody else, as does theirs to you. To add insult to injury, these units carry property taxes 1.8 times higher than phase I units. I have seen phase II units rise in value, but only moderately, and in a downturn you cannot move in to help your cash flow.

d) Hotel-condo units. These units are similar to a phase II covenant in terms of their personal use restrictions. In some earlier developments you are liable only for your mortgage and common-area costs, but newer developments sometimes put buyers on the hook for the performance of restaurants, commercial enterprises, parking spaces, etc.

e) Time-share units. A time-share unit bought on holidays is *not* an investment — it is almost always a self-inflicted financial wound. Why are these units so worthless? Well, first and foremost, the resale market is very difficult. (The secondary market usually operates at less than 50 percent of the original price paid.) And the resort is almost always in competition with you for sales. Think about it, a 200-suite development selling at fifty weeks per unit needs to find 10,000 buyers! The resort will be selling units against you forever. On top of all this, carrying costs can be substantial, often more than the cost of renting a holiday suite. And the "mix and match" approach of trading spaces does not work well. (Most resorts prefer to reserve the best time slots for paying guests rather than trade with you.) If you need to buy one, get a used one. Better yet, don't buy one at all.

The Profit-Seeking Buyer of Vacant Land

The vacant-land buyer is a pure investor. He's not interested in anything but profit. If you're contemplating buying some vacant land, you should ask yourself two main questions. Is inflation likely to make the property more valuable with the passage of time? And is there something I can do to create a profit independent of just waiting for the price of the land to go up?

As a general rule, vacant land simply reflects inflation. But there are a few things you can think about doing to bring yourself out ahead of the game.

a) Buy big and sell small. Large acreage often contains a number of smaller titles. These can be split off and sold separately for a profit.

b) Investigate recreational sub-division potential. Check with local authorities about access requirements, sewage/septic field requirements, minimum allowable lot size, and so forth. Some regions are easy winners for this type of product, but other areas are a tougher play. Time it right and you will make lots of money. Time it wrong and you won't.

c) Buy an axe and a ratty-looking piece of land with potential, and then clean it up. First impressions make a big difference. Pick a weekend during the fall or spring, when the woods are dampish and the fire hazard low, and go in, remove the underbrush, limb the dead bottom branches off the trees, burn the trash, and open the place up to make it more "park-like." It's surprising how much can be done in a couple of weekends — and what a difference it makes on the resale value.

d) Buy land with timber on it and log it to retrieve your purchase price. We advised our newsletter subscribers in 1994 to buy 160-acre parcels in the $25,000 to $50,000 price range. Often, logging only twenty acres of usable timber paid for the whole property.

e) Hire a backhoe and do a big-scale cleanout. As the demand for timber grows, more properties are being privately logged (see above). Once the trees are gone and the profit realized, the owner will often sell the cleared land for a song. When properly cleaned and seeded with grass or replanted with trees, the property can regain some of its former value. It can take real effort, but such land remediation presents a genuine opportunity for profit.

The vacant-land buyer, more than any other kind of real estate investor, will benefit from the clock and the calendar. He's holding his property with the least trouble and at the least cost. And even if there is no monetary inflation, population pressures will make the land more valuable as time passes. This is also a great way to create a portfolio of high-interest first mortgages. Since financing these types of properties is difficult, buyers do not balk at a 12 to 14 percent first mortgage. If you use your RRSP to invest in these mortgages, you are in great return territory.

The Stressed-Out Seeker of Escape

This investor is the rat-race escapee, the seeker of paradise. He sees himself as a Christopher Columbus, sailing into the New World of out-of-town investment. He and his family have been driving real estate prices skywards in the most unlikely places. They can be found in resorts, to be sure, but mostly they look for spots that offer basic amenities, a small-town feeling, and the potential for a new way of life. Yet you must never make the mistake of believing that this person wants to rough it. What he really wants to do is see the cows but not smell them — and of course he needs his sushi.

At one time or another, almost everyone dreams of making the move towards less stress and a more leisurely lifestyle. Today, we are seeing more and more people turn thought into action and actually make the transition. And if what you're looking for is a slower pace, then the average small town has that to offer you. But there are other factors to consider. You may want to look, for example, for areas that show good growth potential with little competition. (In some small towns, you can find opportunities that don't exist in the big cities.) Or if the decision to move is made a little later in life, you probably want to be a little closer to the big city, and thus to entertainment venues, medical services, and anything in between.

The Offshore Escapee

In 1995, our newsletter featured a story headlined "The Cariboo: Where the Deer and the Germans Roam." The article focused on how many prime Canadian farms and ranches, particularly in British Columbia and Nova Scotia, were being snapped up by European and American buyers. Generally, these buyers were looking for not only a good investment at a reasonable price, but also an opportunity to enjoy a "get-away" lifestyle. This trend continues to this day.

Ordinarily, the Chinese buyer is not a seeker of these far-away places; he prefers to go downtown. Still, a number of Chinese investors have financed developments in smaller towns in Ontario, B.C., and Alberta. For their part, Japanese buyers have been huge buyers of resort-type real estate for many years. Unfortunately, the economic turmoil back home has spooked them, and they are no longer prevalent in the marketplace.

The recreational offshore buyer in 2000 and beyond will likely come from the U.S. and Germany. The Euro is not well liked by the average German, so more will be looking offshore for places to invest. The best place to sell property to them is the Internet.

The Opportunist

This is the category that you and I fit into, though unfortunately the word "opportunist" has somehow gained negative connotations over the years. I've never understood why. After all, an opportunist is simply a person who takes advantage of an opening no one else is seizing. For example, an opportunist would look at each of the above buyers and ask, "How can I get there first, buy low, and sell to them at a profit when they come looking?"

Of course, the answer to this question varies depending on the category of buyer you are selling to. But there are some general guidelines you should follow. Let's say, for instance, that you decide you want to be where the "seeker of peace" is going to go. In that case, you should pick a town that has a better-than-average growth rate. The local Statistics Canada office will have a growth-rate chart. Look at it. How is it doing? If the population is shrinking, you should proceed with caution. You'll certainly be able to buy property cheaply, but probably for very good reasons.

Your best bet is to pick a town that has a special reason to grow, such as an incoming highway or new industries. Avoid single-industry towns, especially those that depend on forestry, mining, and fishing. These towns can go from boom to bust almost overnight. All Canadian towns must be able to make the shift from a resource-based economy to an agricultural- or tourism-based one. Look at properties in wine country or other tourist-based areas.

You also want to pick a town that has a good employment base. These businesses are where your tenants are going to come from. If you want to find out what kind of people are moving into a town, get the school enrolment figures. This is often an early indicator of future growth. If elementary school registration is up by 10 percent, this is a promising sign.

Needless to say, two basic principles of real estate investing always apply: 1) you make your most money the day you buy the property; and 2) buy local but sell long distance. What this means is that you yourself have to go to the place where you're considering buying and personally do the shopping around. Trust me, you can save yourself as much as $20,000 or $30,000 by doing this. But when it comes time to sell, you want to sell at a distance. Use multiple listings services and the Internet to expose your product to the big markets.

Finally, be aware that certain facilities and amenities will add value to any investment. Waterfront property of any kind has a special appeal, for example. If you have a property with lake access, that property is going to increase in value over time. And people will pay almost anything to have oceanfront property. Malibu, California, has some of the most expensive real estate in the world, even though every few years a storm comes along and wreaks havoc on people's property.

And of course, there is the magic combination of ocean and island or lake and island. When you combine the lure of the water with the isolation of the island, you get a most appealing combination. This is the one type of property to buy that is virtually a no-lose situation. Even if you pay way too much in the first place, the clock and the calendar will eventually correct your mistake.

Scenic views also get translated into money when it comes to real estate. If you doubt that, then try building the same home in West Vancouver, B.C., and Swan River, Manitoba, and see which one will bring you the highest price. And don't forget about the importance of climate, which doesn't necessarily mean sunshine and warm weather. A large segment of our population likes nothing better than to go up a snow-covered mountain and hurtle back down at breakneck speeds while balanced on two thin pieces of wood. Skiing and other winter sports, as I've said before, are very big attractions.

These are just a few of the factors you should bear in mind when shopping for out-of-town properties. But the main thing — and I can't stress this enough — is to do your due diligence promptly and thoroughly. This is never more important than when you're buying property out of town.

◈

In Essence

> ⟩ If you're thinking of buying out-of-town property, it's crucial that you clearly understand your investment objectives.

◇ Due diligence is particularly important when you're contemplating an out-of-town property.

◇ An opportunist is simply a person who takes advantage of an opening no one else is seizing.

◇ Two basic principles of real estate investing always apply when you're dealing with out-of-town properties: 1) you make the most money on the day you buy; and 2) buy local but sell long distance.

22

Management

*Good management techniques won't make bad people good,
but they will make them behave better.*

Okay, so let's assume now that you've lined up all your ducks in a row and bought yourself a piece of investment real estate. Now that you have it, you have to manage it until you sell it. I'm going to assume here that the readers with large portfolios either have professional managers or have already learned the basics by trial and error. This chapter will be mostly for smaller players or for those just starting out. And I'm going to talk exclusively about income-producing property — that is, something that is rented or leased to an end-user. If you have raw land, there isn't much to manage. All you have to do is look at it every once in a while to make sure that a band of tinkers hasn't set up permanent camp there.

Okay, so you've got your property. If it's already rented, all you have to do is keep a watchful eye on both it and the tenant and make sure that you're charging enough rent. If the property is empty when you take title or if it becomes vacant afterwards, you're going to have the job of getting it rented. For the sake of discussion, I'm going to assume for the rest of this chapter that you're renting a single-family residence — either a house or a condo or an apartment.

No matter what the property, the basic principles for finding new tenants are the same. You'll probably just place an ad in the classifieds of the local weekly paper, and sooner or later the phone will ring and someone will want to see the place. Try to treat your rental like an open house. Advertise that it can be seen only by appointment at certain hours on certain days. If the property is still occupied, it will help to be on good terms with the tenant who is moving out. He will generally be more co-operative and have the place looking better whenever you show it.

When you're showing the property, point out the benefits and tell applicants which faults, if any, you intend to correct (carpets, painting, etc.). Have a rental application prepared and ask interested parties to fill it out. Ask for references and be sure to check them. Don't be timid about this. The only people who are hesitant to give references are those who have something to hide. If you can visit prospective tenants wherever they're currently living, so much the better — this can be a real eye opener.

The better the property you're renting, the more vital it becomes to do a comprehensive credit check. If you don't pay a lot of attention to this step, you're going to be very sorry. The time to address any credit problems with a tenant is before you let that tenant rent. In fact, you're better off letting the place stand empty for a month than you are letting a deadbeat in.

You have to decide at the outset if you're going to be flexible on the rent. For the most part, it's best to accurately determine what the fair market value is and have that as a firm price. If a prospective tenant won't pay that price and you agree to a lesser price, you are likely to have a serious problem when you try to raise the rent later. You are starting out on the wrong foot. You also probably want to avoid tenants who can't really afford the rent. The first time they suffer a financial reversal, you are going to be left holding the bag.

If, however, the market is tough and you are competing for tenants, you may need to be innovative. I generally found it easier to offer real inducements instead of lowering the rent. For example, if your unit has a rental value of $1,000 but high vacancy rates have made the competition lower their rents to $900, try leaving your rent at $1,000 and offering one month free. You are still ahead by $200 a year, and you'll be in a much better position when the market turns. (Note that you want to give the free month at the end of the year, thus assuring that you have a tenant for at least twelve months.) The key is to be innovative.

RENTING TO OWN

Let's say you want to sell your property and you have a long-term tenant who has expressed an interest in buying. This tenant, however, is a little strapped for cash and says, "Look, we'd like to buy this house but we have no cash for a down payment. If you'll sign over the house, we'll pay you the down payment in three years." If the market's bad or you don't especially need the money, this may sound okay to you. But if you don't listen to anything else I've told you, listen to this: never, ever sign over your property with no money down to anyone. By all means, buy for no money down if you can, but never sell under those conditions. Times change, circumstances change. What happens if the tenant loses his job, or answers the call of the wild? It is extremely costly and time-consuming to repossess a property if the buyer had no original equity.

What you can do is offer your long-term tenant — or anyone else you think is reliable — a rent-to-own deal. Let's say the house is valued at $100,000 and the rental value of the property is $1,000 per month. Under the terms of the deal, your tenant will pay the $1,000 a month, plus $200 extra. In return, you give him the option to buy the house for a fixed price on a fixed day. The accumulated $200 per month will be applied against the total down payment due.

To continue the example, let's say the contract is written with an option for thirty months, at which time the tenant can buy. He now has $6,000 ($200 x 30), and decides to use $5,000 for the down payment. He can get a CMHC first mortgage for the rest, and he can use the extra thousand for the transfer costs and fees. It's a no-lose situation for you, because if the tenant does not exercise the option for any reason, his $6,000 is forfeited (after all, you effectively took the property off the market for him). Of course, you'll want to use a good lawyer to draw up the option agreement. A verbal contract isn't worth the paper it's printed on.

A LANDLORD'S WORK IS NEVER DONE

You should also always use a rental agreement. If you don't have your own, use a standard form — just make sure you have everything in writing. You never want to take legal action if you can possibly avoid it, but having a strong rental agreement allows you to make convincing threats.

So how much rent should you charge? Sometimes it's hard to know how high you can go without hurting the rentability. My feeling is that it's better to be a few dollars below the market than a few dollars above it. If you're overpriced by even one dollar, your unit won't rent. This is why it's important to keep surveying the neighbourhood's comparable units. These comparables are your competition, and an accurate assessment of this competition is going to tell you what you can charge.

Next, you have to decide what you're going to allow and what you're not going to allow. Children and pets, for example, are hard on property. (There are always exceptions, but at the end of a year's tenancy, a piece of property that had kids and pets will generally be worth less than the same property without.) If you permit them, you're going to have to allow for more wear and tear. I'm not making a recommendation one way or the other — I think it's an individual choice — but you should be aware of the potential problems and plan accordingly.

Now, every now and again, you will check a potential tenant's references, run a credit check, visit him at his existing home, and still end up renting to a troublemaker. When that happens, you have to deal with it right away. When it comes to property management, problems do not get better and they *never* go away by themselves. They always get worse and multiply. Nip them in the bud, if you can, because the first loss you take is always the smallest.

This means that if you have a "no pet" rule and your tenant gets a cute little kitten that is just too precious for words, you have to be the villain. If you don't, the next pet might be a massive boa constrictor that will escape and curl up behind the dryer in the laundry room and put that nice little eighty-three-year-old widow on the third floor into near cardiac arrest. (I mention this only because it actually happened to a friend of mine.)

Or let's say the rent is due on the last day of every month and one month your tenant's a day late. No big deal, right? Wrong. If you don't put your foot down right away, the next month it will be five days late. (I believe that people make a conscious choice about who to disappoint when it comes to being late with money. And they will invariably disappoint the nicest person because this is the easiest and most pleasant course of action. I arrange things so that the last person on their list of people to disappoint is me, and I suggest you do likewise.)

Unfortunately, every once in a while the dice are going to fall the wrong way for you because they fell the wrong way for your tenant. When this happens, late rent will turn into no rent, and you'll have to get them out of there. This is where it helps if you have established a good relationship and it can be kept friendly. If it can't, you'll have to go through the eviction process, which you'll want to keep as expeditious as possible.

Making things easy at the end is another reason to take care at the beginning. We've all heard horror stories about people renting to bikers who completely trashed the property before moving out. You avoid this problem by not renting to questionable tenants in the first place.

I have owned my share of rental properties, and I have both good and bad stories to tell. In my experience, though, the easiest way to get into trouble is to mix up your own objectives. Most of us want a tenant who will pay off our mortgage, pay on time every time, maintain the property better than if it was his own, and still love us unconditionally. Well, I have news for you. You'll get some of these qualities some of the time, but not all of these qualities all of the time. And the most dangerous of these is wanting to be loved by your tenant. This just isn't possible — after all, the two of you are at cross-purposes. He wants to pay as little as possible, with you shouldering all of the upkeep; you want him to pay as much as possible and cut the grass too. But do the best you can to stay on good terms. All the joy of ownership goes out the window when landlord-tenant relationships go sour.

PROPERTY MANAGERS

Unless you actually live within easy reach of all of those far-flung revenue properties, you're going to be relying on someone else to manage things. Once again, it's important that you do your research thoroughly and choose a professional who is capable of handling the job. Think about it for a minute. The average investor owns his property for six years. The average single-family home rental value in Vancouver is $1,500 a month, or $18,000 a year. That's a cool $108,000 spread over that six-year period. This is serious money, and it needs to be managed seriously. Matter-of-fact management companies that will rent to anyone have ended up cracking many an investment egg.

So what does a service-oriented property manager do, anyway? Well, he provides a *written* budget outline, income projections, simple accounting and bookkeeping, and property maintenance. He also ensures the timely collection of rent, controls expenses, and helps establish rental value, when necessary.

Before you hire a manager, have him show you the operating procedure he employs for maintenance (ongoing action or reaction to problems as they occur only), repairs (ditto), safety and security issues (how? when? who?), and insurance (enough to ensure that all eventualities are covered). You should also inspect the property together and go over his regular (weekly, daily, monthly) inspection routine. Make certain that he understands the scope of his authority. Does he hire contractors to do needed work? Does he advance funds? Does he use rental income to place ads? Does he make his own repairs? What is his track record? Who can you call to verify?

If you do this all up front and have a *written understanding of your relationship*, you will have established a basis for measuring actual performance against promised performance.

Of course, it doesn't end there. After you've hired a professional manager, you then have to manage the manager. You have to be eternally vigilant so that you'll know when he has stopped doing what he's supposed to be doing as soon as he has stopped doing it. Remember that the better you or your manager perform the management functions, the more you will gross and the less you will spend. And of course, whatever you don't spend is what you get to keep. And that, after all, is the reason we play the game.

In Essence

> The time to address any potential problems with a tenant is before you let that tenant move in.

◇ You never want to take legal action if you can possibly avoid it, but having a strong rental agreement allows you to make convincing threats.

◇ It's better to be a few dollars below the market than a few dollars above it.

◇ The joy of ownership goes out the window when landlord-tenant relationships go sour.

◇ A good manager will save you money, but a bad one will cost you money.

23

Income Tax

[In] this world nothing can be said to be certain, except death and taxes.

— BENJAMIN FRANKLIN

Everything there is to say on the subject of income taxes has already been said. "Only a damn fool pays income tax!" said Bernard Baruch. And Will Rogers famously quipped, "Don't give money to politicians. It only encourages them!" But I don't really need to come up with anything new to say because I know that I am preaching to the converted. I have yet to meet anyone who thinks that taxes are too low, or that the government needs more of our money because it is doing such a good job with what it is getting now.

Still, for the time being at least, we all have to continue paying taxes. So it may help a little to understand what they are all about. First, let's deal with the philosophy of income tax. The idea all started when two families got together and decided to put a protective fence around their huts. The dominant male said, "I'm going to be in charge of building this fence and maintaining it, but I don't see why I should have to pay for it myself. So that everything will be fair, everybody protected by the fence is going to have to kick in a share." And everybody kicked in a share and everything was fair. They decided to call this payment a tax.

One day, the dominant male thought it would be a good idea to put up a statue to himself, and so the tax had to be increased to cover the cost of the statue. People complained that the dominant male was spending money foolishly when there were people starving, so the dominant male had to send over a policeman to bop them on the head until the complaining stopped. Naturally, the cost of the policeman had to be covered by an increase in taxes.

Now, there were two kinds of people in the village: those who had property and made money and those who had nothing and needed things. At first, the dominant male made slaves out of the people who had nothing. But then some genius discovered that economic slavery was way better than the kind with whips and chains. The dominant male decided to enslave the productive segment of society by taxing its members just enough to keep the government going and yet not so much that they would rise up in armed revolt.

The whole exercise was like fishing with a cormorant, a bird that is great at catching fish. A smart fisherman will catch a cormorant, tie a string around its leg, put a ring around its neck, and let it sit on the edge of his boat. When the bird sees a fish swim by, it dives down and tries to swallow it, but the ring around its neck keeps the fish from going down all the way. The fisherman pulls on the string and hauls the cormorant, together with the fish, back into the boat. Then he retrieves the fish and perches the cormorant on the edge of the boat until the next one swims by and the process starts all over again. Every once in a while, the fisherman removes the ring from around the cormorant's neck and the bird gets to eat a fish. That's how he stays interested in the game.

And here we have very accurately described the relationship between the productive taxpayer and the taxman. If you'd like to have more money to spend on yourself, all you've got to do is figure out how to swallow more of the fish before the fisherman gets to them.

TAX AVOIDANCE IS THE KEY

Most sensible people agree that we have to have roads and schools, a police force, and probably even an army. Widows and the aged must be cared for, and children must have milk. But what we don't always agree on is the best way to accomplish this. There is a school of thought that says that if you let people who make money keep that money, they will then use that money to make more money, thus raising the standard of living for the country as a whole. There is another school of thought that says that if you give all the money to the government, politicians will use it to create a heaven here on earth. The answer, of course, lies somewhere in between these two schools, but I believe it's probably a lot closer to the first than the second.

The people who pay the least taxes and therefore keep most of the money they earn for themselves are also the people who consider themselves to be at war with the tax department. The best weapon you can have in this war is a constant awareness that the war is going on. This doesn't mean you're going to be a bad citizen. It just means that you're not going to pay any unnecessary taxes. Indeed, Judge Learned Hand of the U.S. Supreme Court has said that it is a person's right to arrange his affairs so as to pay the least tax possible. This is what's known as tax avoidance. You must never engage in tax evasion, which is illegal.

If you believe, as I do, that governments will be more efficient if we give them less, then you have a duty as a citizen to hang on to as much of your money as possible. Politicians spend your tax money to buy your vote. If you don't think this is the reality, then you should be drawing pictures with a crayon and affixing them to the side of the refrigerator with a magnet. Bureaucrats spend your tax money because their success is measured in the size of their budget. And any of their budget that is not spent is returned to the treasury, and that amount is deducted from what they are given in the following year. Can you guess what they are going to do with any money that looks like it might be left over?

Each dollar that you don't pay tax on is really one dollar doing the work of two. So every time you earn a dollar, you should see if there is a way to take that dollar as anything other than income. And every time you spend a dollar, you should see if there is a way to make that expenditure deductible from your income. Some people even strive to make every breath they take tax deductible. If they buy a stick of chewing gum, they give half of it to a prospective client so they can write it off. They establish a home-based business so they can write off a portion of their mortgage payments. Their home-based business provides them with a Cadillac Eldorado for their business calls. They save every scrap of paper and document every transaction for that fateful day when the taxman decides to audit.

The key to winning the war with the taxman, particularly for the real estate investor, is to have a sound record-keeping system right off the bat. If you are properly documented and have a logical rationale for even an aggressive tax posture, you will not present an attractive target to the taxman. Remember that he is running a money factory, and that every person in every department of that factory has to produce a certain amount. If you are not an attractive target, the taxman is going to pass you by and concentrate on someone he can beat up more easily.

In fact, when it comes to being a target, you want to be as unappealing as possible. This is why you don't want to be a do-it-yourselfer when it comes to preparing your taxes. Having a good tax professional standing between you and the tax department makes you about as appealing as a wet dog on a hot day. But remember that being well documented carries more weight than the letterhead of your accounting firm. And it is these documents, and not your tax professional, that will protect you if you are audited.

If you have all the documentation you need to back your claim, you can be as creative as you want — within reason. I once heard of a cab driver who claimed his uniforms as a business expense. The taxman disallowed the deduction on the grounds that the driver needed clothes anyway. The next year, he again claimed the cost of his uniforms, but this time he described them as seat covers. The deduction was passed without anyone batting an eye.

Don't be afraid to put a little pressure on your accountant if you feel he's not doing enough to help you avoid taxes. I know someone whose accountant prepared a return that showed he owed a considerable amount. The man said to his tax preparer, "You don't seem to understand. I have money for income tax and I have money for your fee, but I don't have money for both." The tax preparer recalculated the numbers, and soon both the return and his bill were almost nil.

THE LAST WORD

In the real estate investment world, there are a hundred things to know about write-offs, taking appropriate deductions, and calculating taxes payable. This is why you need professional advice. Fortunately, your written business plan makes it easy. If you go to a professional, tell him what you want to do, and ask how to position yourself before you start, you will soon be as tax-effective as possible. In the end, it's all a matter of how creative, well-documented, and logical your premise is. Ultimately, the person who is the most aggressive will usually pay the least tax.

In Essence

◇ If you let people who make money keep that money, they will generally make more money, thus raising the standard of living for everyone else.

◇ The best weapon you can have in the war against the tax department is a constant awareness that the war is going on.

◇ Each dollar that you don't pay tax on is really one dollar doing the work of two.

◇ The key to winning the war with the taxman, particularly for the real estate investor, is to always keep good records.

◇ When it comes to being a target for the taxman, you want to make yourself as unappealing as possible.

24

What to Buy and What Not to Buy

I'm a great believer in luck, and I find the harder I work, the more luck I have.

— *Thomas Jefferson*

For six years, I have published a highly detailed sixteen-page monthly newsletter and a weekly two-page fax for several thousand subscribers. I hold six in-house subscriber seminars and speak at more than one hundred events per year. I analyze, debate, and study in detail any and all aspects of real estate investment. But in the end, it always boils down to this: "Okay, okay, Ozzie, I understand. But now tell me exactly what should I buy and where."

We all lead busy lives, and so it's never a surprise to me that people would rather have me advise them than do all the legwork themselves.

And that is why I wrote this chapter on what to buy and what to avoid. Before we begin, however, I'd like to add a disclaimer or two.

If you have learned nothing else from this book, you do probably realize that the real estate market is always changing. Let me give you an example of this. In 1993, we identified for our newsletter subscribers a number of small towns in which to invest, one of which was Courtenay, B.C. At the time, vacancy rates there were falling, big retailers were moving in, and the population was growing. In fact, by 1996 Courtenay had the highest population growth in the province. Yet by the summer of 1994, we had placed Courtenay on investor alert. Developers had moved in in droves, driving up property prices to almost twice their former levels. For us, it was time to leave. Knowing when to get out is just as important as knowing when to get in.

The same thing happened with Whistler. We had long been leery about some types of investment property there, but we had nevertheless recommended the resort for years. It had all the best reasons to invest: strong population growth, huge capital investment, a rating as the top ski resort in the world. But in February 1997, thanks to overbuilding and vastly overvalued properties, we placed Whistler on investor alert, just as we had done with Courtenay three years earlier.

We forecast price increases of 20 percent for Toronto in 1996 and 10 percent for Calgary in 1997 and 1998. Yet by the time you read this, we may well have changed direction again. The point is that no high stays high forever and no low stays low forever. You can no longer simply count on inflation to bail you out if you make a buying mistake. Some property classes will rise in value, and others will fall at the same time in the same marketplace. Change is the only constant. *Caveat emptor.*

REMEMBER THE BASICS

1. As an investor in a new home, you need to buy at least 12 percent below market value. Let's say you buy a home for $400,000. When you add GST of $28,000, land-transfer taxes of $5,000 or so (this

varies by area), and $14,500 in commission when you sell it, you'll see that you need to sell the property for $447,500 just to break even.

2. In most markets in Canada, sales volume in the first six months of the year is 60 percent of the volume of the last six months. It is better to sell in the spring.

3. In most markets in Canada, prices peak in May and drop in December and January. Usually it's best to buy in a low and sell in a peak, but there are exceptions.

4. In small towns and northern areas, prices rise after the winter goes and drop when the first snow falls.

5. Single-family homes have outperformed townhouses and condominiums every time and for every market. No matter which city we look at — Vancouver, Toronto, Calgary, Edmonton, etc. — single-family homes have shown greater price appreciation over time. The difference is in the land; Canadians still like to have a place to put their barbecues. This may change, however, in those cities where condos outsell single-family homes. In Edmonton and Calgary, condominium sales account for only 18 percent of the market; 72 percent of sales are still in single-family homes. In Vancouver, however, condos now account for more than 50 percent of all sales. And of course, wherever the greater number of people want to trade, price appreciation follows.

6. Ground-oriented townhouse units generally outperform high-rise condos.

7. New condominiums depreciate, but used condominiums appreciate (unless you buy in high-inflationary times).

8. Be careful not to pay too much for higher floors in a high-rise. Let's say you buy into a building that's twenty-five storeys high. Unless you're buying the penthouse, don't pay more for "view." Once you are what realtors call "in view" — usually the twelfth floor and above — it makes no sense to pay more money for a suite one floor higher. I have seen developers add as much as $2,000 a floor "because you get better views," but it is wasted money for the

investor. Once you are in view, resale buyers will not pay anything extra to be a little higher.

9. You don't make any money buying foreclosures. Foreclosures sound sexy, but they are an investor graveyard of wasted time and effort. I have seen very, very few foreclosures work for the investor.

10. Tax sales are only a fad. There are very few (if any) Canadian investors who have consistently made money off tax sales. In the United States, where the laws are much tougher on people who owe back taxes, there are some great bargains to be had. But in Canada this approach works only rarely.

11. Cities in which the government is the major employer should be avoided. We voters are so disenchanted with our governments that we want them to downsize. Downsizing means fewer employees, and fewer employees means properties are sold and markets fall. We placed Edmonton, Ottawa, and Victoria on investor alert in 1995 for this very reason.

12. A good location is never more important than timing and trends. You can always make more money faster if you get in at the beginning of an up-cycle or you identify a powerful new trend.

WHAT TO BUY

1. Your own single-family home.
2. Single-family homes with basement suites anywhere in the country.
3. Two- to five-year-old downtown condos in major cities, preferably on water or a park.
4. Any waterfront property. It will always appreciate within its timing cycle.
5. Major resort properties with unlimited personal use.
6. Mini-warehouses. With the trend to self-employment, more and more small companies are looking for their own space. The hot spots will be suburbs or cities where they allow a larger component of office space (more than 15 percent) in an industrial warehouse.

If you can swing it, buy an existing industrial park, spruce it up, and get more and more office space converted.

7. Mini-storage parks. As more families downsize and move out of town, mini-storage parks will become increasingly attractive. This is a strong real estate play, with good cash flow and low overhead.

8. Small apartment buildings or strip malls. Snap these up while REITs are still in a buying mode, helping to drive prices higher. The competition will drive values far beyond the underlying revenue streams.

WHERE TO BUY

1. Casino towns. Values will climb in those casino towns that also have strong capital investment, high employment, a thriving tourism industry, etc.

2. Major markets that are experiencing a downturn. Some used condos in downtown Vancouver, for example, have been discounted by up to 40 percent.

3. Small towns in Alberta, B.C., and Ontario that have:
   a) better-than-average population growth;
   b) vacancy rates at or below 4 percent;
   c) a new highway, new employment, or some other reason to grow;
   d) good prices (especially if you can buy with a low down payment yet still have good cash flow);
   e) competent available property managers;
   f) more than one industry;
   g) university or college with character.

WHAT NOT TO BUY

1. Hotel-type limited-use units in resorts and time-share units of any kind.

2. Properties in small towns that are lacking the features listed above.
3. Limited partnerships that you can't break.
4. Property that is situated on or abuts Native land. Some resort owners have seen the values of their land depreciate by 50 percent because of roadblocks and other turmoil. At the present time, I would advise you to stay away from these kinds of properties. But if you're hell-bent on proceeding, make sure that the development you're interested in has a head-lease in place with the Department of Indian Affairs in Ottawa. Otherwise, you'll have little protection if trouble starts.
5. Property that has bad feng shui. I know, I know, some of you will think I have gone bonkers. But if you reside on the West Coast, with its many new Asian immigrants, you would be well advised to note a few feng shui basics. The Chinese believe that where you live and how you allocate and arrange the elements of your home or workplace can significantly affect your health, wealth, and happiness. Seemingly simple things such as improperly placed furniture, incorrect colour schemes, and elemental conflicts (for example, having the "water," or refrigerator, next to the "fire," or stove) can create factors that impact negatively on your life. So if you think your likely future buyer will be of Chinese descent, you may want to avoid such things as straight roads leading directly to the home, dead ends and cul-de-sacs, heavy beams, and the number four.

Of course, I could go on and on. But the main thing to remember is that the market is changing all the time. If and when inflation visibly returns, you may be able to buy anything anywhere and do well with it. Until then, look over some of the suggestions I've listed above and pick your best bets.

◇

In Essence

◇ Single-family homes have outperformed townhouses and condominiums every time and in every market.

◇ New condominiums depreciate, but used condominiums appreciate.

⟩ It's a myth that there is money to be made on foreclosures and tax sales.

⟩ A good location is never more important than timing and trends, though waterfront property will always be valuable.

25

What to Do When the Rains Come

Life experience teaches that we generally get back what we put out. If we do not like what we are getting back, we should examine what we are putting out.

— ERIC ACCENBAUGH

This chapter is about an aspect of the real estate business that you almost never hear discussed, and that is what to do when the bad times come. Any damn fool can survive good times. What separates the grown-ups from the children is how you handle the trouble.

The problem is that it's almost impossible to get enough experience at handling trouble to become adept at it. When you get into trouble in real estate investing, you either lose all your money and are forced out of the game, or you are so traumatized by the experience that you take all your money and walk away from the game. Therefore, to learn about trouble at a point when it's going to do you some good, you're going to have to benefit from the experiences of people who have walked the road before you. Anyway, this is not the kind of thing you want to learn first-hand if you can possibly avoid it.

Earlier in this book, we learned that one of the secrets of success is to find prosperous people and have them tell us their tricks of the trade. It stands to reason that the same course of action would work if we wanted to know about failure. We should seek out people who have failed and get them to tell us what went wrong. But because human nature is what it is, people who have failed find that there isn't too much call for their consulting services.

It's also really too bad that they don't teach this anywhere in school. You can go out there and get a degree in commerce and a Master of Business Administration, you can study for years and read hundreds of textbooks and learn from dozens of professors, but not one of those textbooks or one of those professors is going to tell you what to do when you find yourself in trouble that you can't get out of.

THE THREE CATEGORIES OF TROUBLE

So when we talk about trouble, just what is it that we're talking about? Well, for our purposes, trouble is anything that is going to cost you money. In general, this kind of trouble can be broken down into three categories: 1) things you do to yourself; 2) things other people do to you; and 3) things that just happen.

If you have to get into trouble, the best kind is the trouble you bring on yourself. This is because you have the power to stop it as soon as you realize what's causing it. Let's say, for example, that you decide there is a market in providing rental accommodation to biker gangs, so you pursue that market and rent one of your houses to some bikers. Almost before the ink is dry on the rental agreement, however, they have painted the house purple and littered the front yard with old motorcycle parts and are refusing to pay you any rent. You have to evict them and cover over the purple paint and get rid of the junk and start all over.

Before you had the actual experience, the idea of renting to biker gangs seemed like a good one. Because there wasn't much supply available to them, it appeared that you could ask a higher rent and have the market pretty much to yourself. Once you'd rented that first house, however, the idea suddenly didn't seem so attractive. But because this was trouble you'd caused yourself, all you had to do was stop renting to bikers and the problem was solved.

The second category of trouble covers things other people do to you. Let's say that you have a partner whose job it is to act as manager of your portfolio of properties. In this scenario, this manager is the one who decides to rent the property to the bikers. The end result is the same, but now there is someone else to blame — or is there? Is the mistake his for renting to the bikers, or is it your mistake because you chose him as your partner and gave him that responsibility in the first place? Where does the buck stop?

Trouble that falls into the third category is usually the most costly, but because we can put it down to simple "bad luck," it's also the easiest to bear. Let's say that, to continue the example we used above, the government decides it wants to pass a law forcing you to rent your property to biker gangs. Once again, the end result is the same, but this time there was nothing you could have done about it. You have no choice but to shake your fist at the sky in well-justified rage.

It's my opinion that an inordinate amount of bad luck comes to us from the government. Now, there is a school of thought that says that people get the kind of government they deserve. But that outlook does not give a whole lot of comfort to someone caught up in the coils of some mindless, faceless, brainless, and heartless bureaucracy. And of course, whenever you give authority without personal responsibility, you are going to create a potential brick wall for the investor. Taxmen, securities regulators, by-law inspectors, zoning officials — any one of these people can ruin you. But being able to identify the source of your difficulties doesn't really matter if it doesn't help you avoid them.

The costs and consequences are the same.

I once overheard a conversation in a repair shop while I was waiting for my car. The service manager was explaining to a customer why the mistake he had made was not his fault. The customer responded, "Look, I pay for my mistakes. If you have someone who pays for yours, please tell me who it is so I can continue this conversation with him!" My point? If you're the one who has to pay, it doesn't matter whose fault it is.

HOW TO RECOGNIZE WHEN YOU'RE IN TROUBLE

In the real estate game, it's fairly easy to figure out when you're in trouble. It happens when you have more money going out than you have coming in, or when your property is sinking in value like a stone, or when you have amounts due but no money to pay them, or, or, or, or . . .

The warning signs will eventually become clear, and when they do you need to act quickly. Remember the third golden rule that is carved over the door to the Ozzie Jurock College of Knowledge: the sooner you take a loss, the smaller that loss will be. (The first two golden rules, of course, are "Forget about location, location, location" and "You make the most money on the day you buy the property.")

For example, let's say you own a small apartment building and the rental market has collapsed. If your business plan states that you aren't concerned with making a capital gain, you may be tempted to wait out the bad times. But if things go seriously against you — if, for instance, three of the six units are empty and you do not have the wherewithal to subsidize them — then you had better sell.

The big trick is to recognize trouble for what it is and then have the wisdom and the courage to take the necessary steps. This is where human nature is our own worst enemy. Often, we run into what I call emotional cost accounting.

Generally, people have two different approaches to losses. The realists consider a loss to have occurred the moment it actually happened. Let's say, for instance, that you buy a stock on Monday for a hundred dollars. If it's worth ninety dollars on Tuesday, the realist will say that he lost 10 percent. But the emotional cost accountant will say, "I paid a hundred dollars for this, and as long as I hold it in my portfolio and don't sell it, I will not actually have suffered *any* loss."

The real difference between these two approaches is how they affect a person's course of action. Because the realist is in a position to recognize the loss on the day it starts, he can limit it to 10 percent by selling the stock right away. The emotional cost accountant, by contrast, takes comfort in the delusion that the loss hasn't happened yet and props this up with the hope that his stock will recover. He feels in his heart that this investment now "owes" him ten dollars. He will look you in the eye and, with a straight face, say, "I can't sell this stock until it comes back to what I paid for it." And he will stick to this position even if the stock drops from ninety dollars to ten cents.

Whether the problem is bad luck or bad judgement, the results are always the same. That's why the sooner you recognize trouble, the sooner you can exercise whatever damage control is possible. And this need for damage control underscores, once again, the importance of having a *written* business plan. If you have a detailed plan that you constantly consult and update, you're going to know as soon as it is possible to know when you are not meeting your benchmarks. You're going to know as soon as it's possible to know when problems are going to require your attention. And although this may not make the problem any easier to solve, it does go a long way towards minimizing the damage.

A friend of mine once spent a summer as the director of a day camp. He tells me it was the most stressful job he ever had. There were forty-two six-year-olds enrolled at the camp, and all he did all day long was count from one to forty-two over and over again. Whenever the total was forty or forty-one, everyone stopped what they were doing and went looking for the missing kids. Once they found them, my friend would go back to his counting.

The same principle can be applied to your real estate investments. The closer you watch them and the more you measure them against your written plan, the sooner you will know when something has gone wrong and the faster you'll be able to implement damage control. The sooner you start looking for the missing six-year-olds, in other words, the better off you're going to be.

Unfortunately, there will come a time when the trouble is severe enough that you will have to have some help. When the wolves start to snap at your heels, you need to place some intermediaries between you and the people who are harassing you. Your accountant, if his expertise is in this area, can buy you time and breathing room. But the person who can buy you the most breathing room is your lawyer. That's why choosing the right professionals at the outset is so important.

When things are at their very worst, you may have to play the bankruptcy card. For this, there is no question that you are going to have to use the services of an expert. But make sure you get a good one, because he can make all the difference in the world. I once saw two partners go bankrupt in the same deal. One of them did it the wrong way and wound up losing everything that it was possible to lose, including his wife. The other got a good bankruptcy lawyer and managed to keep his house, his vacation place, his boat, and a couple of very expensive cars. That his marriage stood up under the strain was probably just a coincidence, but who knows for sure?

Let me give you one other piece of advice about bankruptcy: if it has to happen, then it can't happen soon enough. Any stalling you do is dead time in your life, because you can't move on until the process is over and done with. I know one person who dragged out his bankruptcy for three and a half years. In that time, the lawyers and the accountants made a small fortune, the creditors got slightly less than they would have if things had proceeded in a timely fashion, and the bankrupt investor was in limbo for three and a half of what should have been the most productive years of his life. If you ever find yourself in that position, don't make the same mistake.

In these kinds of situations, it's important to bear in mind that the only thing you're going to lose is money. Of course, most people think losing their money is the end of the world, but I feel it's all a question of perspective. As long as you don't make yourself sick over the situation, you're going to come out the other side in one piece, ready to start again. The key is to survive psychologically.

Everybody has his own way of dealing with these matters, and your reactions are going to be dictated in large measure by whatever personal philosophy you've developed. Someone who goes broke once and then quits is easy to understand. What's a little more difficult to grasp is how a person could fail more than once, start all over again, and continue in the game. Yet I know many people like this, and they almost all share qualities of optimism and resilience.

Still, the "repeat offenders" I have known have never suffered the same kind of failure twice. Indeed, there are many who've made no mistakes at all and have only been the victims of bad luck. If you play the game often enough, it is not unreasonable to expect that you too may run into some bad luck along the way.

Let's say, for example, that you're just an average investor who decides to buy a Vancouver condo as an investment. It's a nice and conservative investment, and a few years down the road, after your kids leave home, you'll have the option of selling your house and moving into this condo. All in all, it seems to make a lot of sense.

But you are a prudent investor, so you proceed to do all kinds of investigating. First, you check out the neighbourhood. It's good. You check out the past history of the builder and the architect and the developer. All good. You check the realtor and learn that 90 percent of the units have been sold. You do all the comparisons and examinations you can think of, and all of the answers you get are positive. Then — and only then — do you plunk down your money and become a proud condo owner.

But the day after your cheque is cashed, someone in the building reports a leak. Then another. Then another. There are strata council meetings. People thump on the table and beat their breasts and fingers are pointed and committees are appointed. It turns out that the building is leaking like a sieve, and that once the water gets in, it can't get out. Everything is going all mouldy. Pretty soon, the amount needed to fix the problem is more than what you owe on the mortgage. Your money is irrevocably lost, and yet you did everything right. This comes under the heading of plain, ordinary, garden-variety bad luck.

And the bad luck doesn't stop there. Down the street is another project just like yours. Same architect, same builder — the only difference is that this project came along three months later and now, with all the bad ink in the newspapers about leaky condos, the developer can't sell any of his units. His lender gets tired of waiting for the construction loan to be repaid, so he forecloses. And because the developer, as a matter of course, signed a personal guarantee, he is going to wind up bankrupt. Bad luck all around.

THE LAST WORD

When you get into trouble, what is really important is that you recognize the problem quickly, do what you can to mitigate the effects, salvage whatever you're able to, and do as much as you can to preserve the relationships you've established. And then tell yourself that it's only money. If you maintain a positive attitude, you'll come through the crisis only slightly battered and bruised — and usually ready to start again.

In Essence

⬦ To learn about trouble at a point where it's going to do you some good, you're going to have to benefit from the experiences of people who have walked the road before you.

⬦ Bad luck is often the most costly kind of trouble, but it's also the easiest to bear.

> The sooner you take a loss, the smaller that loss will be.

> Don't delude yourself into thinking that a loss hasn't happened just because it hasn't shown up on your balance sheet yet.

⬦ If bankruptcy has to happen, it can't happen soon enough.

⬦ It's never too late to start again.

Epilogue

Ah, but a man's reach should exceed his grasp,
Or what's a heaven for?
— ROBERT BROWNING, "ANDREA DEL SARTO"

In this book, I have done my best to cover the entire spectrum of the real estate investment business. I wish I could tell you that you now know everything you need to know about it, but the fact of the matter is that I've just scratched the surface. To deal with some of these issues in any real depth, I'd need to write twenty-six books instead of twenty-six chapters. But what I have done is describe the field and point out some areas where you should focus your attention. And I've also told you some things about this business that you won't find written down anywhere else.

It took me a lifetime to learn what's in this book. A lot of it I learned from personal experience, but most of it I learned from the examples of those who had travelled the road before me. That is, without question, the most effective, efficient way to acquire knowledge. And since I've been everything from a one-man real estate operation to the president of the largest real estate brokerage company in Canada, I've had a chance to observe every kind of success and every kind of failure. I've taken what I consider to be the important elements of these observations and put them in this book along with an attempt to explain why and how they happened. So if I was going to teach a young person what she should know about real estate investment, the following are the points I would stress.

1. *About 10 percent of what people do is action and the other 90 percent is reaction.* People let circumstances dictate their behaviour. While I believe that people would have a lot more choice if they only sat down, planned more, and reacted less, life for most people is not like this.

   But even if you're a person who acts from choice only 10 percent of the time, make sure that all that action is focused on activities that will make you grow. At the end of twenty years, you want to be a person with twenty years' experience, not a person who has had one year of experience twenty times over.

2. *Remember the basics; they aren't difficult to grasp.* In real estate investing, the premise at the core of everything is that you make the most money on the day you buy the property. Once you've learned this premise, you must ask the necessary questions, seek out the required answers, interpret the information you get, and take the necessary actions.

   Be a good listener. God gave you two ears and one mouth for a reason. Don't assume anything, and always look for win/win situations.

3. *Timing is crucial.* You want to be selling when others are buying and buying when others are selling. And never forget that the market is *always* changing. You have to know when those changes are affecting your properties, so that you're ready to act when necessary. Whether you're a big investor or a small investor, ignorance will cost you real money. It is a matter only of degree, not of kind.

4. *The small investor has the advantage of flexibility. The large investor has the advantage of muscle.* You should always try to play to your opponent's weaknesses and get him to play to your strengths, but to do this you need to understand what those strengths and weaknesses are. Understanding yourself can turn you from a small investor into a large one.

5. *There is nothing more important than putting your personal real estate investment plan into writing.* A written plan will, at the beginning of your career, help you define what kind of a player you are, which in turn will help you determine what kind of games to play. Commit yourself to a plan of action, and then use it to measure your results.

   A written plan will also help you define what your expectations are, and it will map a route from where you are to where you want to be. You will always know what your next step is, and thus will always be directing your energies exactly where you should be.

6. *The money you don't lose is twice as important as the money you win.* This is Economics 101. If you start with a dollar and make another dollar, you'll be one dollar ahead. If you lose that dollar, however, you'll have to make two dollars the next time just to come out even. Remember that the very best way to deal with trouble is to stay out of it. It doesn't matter how many good deals you say no to, as long as you don't say yes to a bad one.

7. *In any negotiation, the person who cares least is going to have a large advantage.* The best tool you can have in the negotiating process is

detached knowledge of the market. And never forget that the buyer is *always* the one who ultimately sets the price. Still, if you are winning a negotiation, make sure you allow the other person to save some face. Sometimes it's better not to try to wring out the last dollar; you could negotiate yourself right out of the deal.

8. *Beware the naysayers.* The world has changed and is continuing to change. And no one can say for sure what the future holds. Had you listened to all the dire predictions of 1961, 1974, 1981, 1982, 1983, 1986, and 1988 and not bought a house, you would have done a serious disservice to yourself and your family. If you had listened to the prognostications of demographers in 1995, you would have missed the 20 percent house price increase in Toronto and the 9.5 to 20 percent increase in most major cities in the U.S.

All this is why I like to say that there are no good and bad markets — only good and bad deals. I have seen some absolutely terrible deals made in some of the very best markets, and vice versa. Don't listen to all the doom and gloom. The bottom line is that real estate ownership is the greatest wealth builder for individuals of all time. It always has been and it always will be.

These are some of the more important points to impress on your children and grandchildren, but first you must make sure that you have impressed them on yourself. There isn't any big secret to making money by investing in real estate. There isn't even any big trick to it. All you have to possess are the relatively ordinary qualities of hard work, ingenuity, resourcefulness, and care. And then you have to put those qualities to work.

I wish you luck in your adventures.

Index